OUT
SPOKEN
PRESS

Published by Out-Spoken Press,
Future Studio,
237 Hackney Road,
London, E2 8NA

A CIP record for this title is available from the British Library.

First edition published 2017
ISBN: 978-0-9931038-9-6

Artwork:
Ben Lee

Printed & Bound by:
Print Resource

Typeset in: Baskerville

Out-Spoken Press is supported using public funding by the National Lottery through Arts Council England.

SONGS MY ENEMY TAUGHT ME

Contents

Introduction

'...for the female is, as it were, a mutilated male'
— Aristotle, Generation of Animals

Songs My Enemy Taught Me is a collection of poems themed around the experiences of women globally, but it had simple beginnings. It began with me. It began with a small child in a hotel room not wanting to speak. It began with opera, but the kind that cannot be heard. It began at the point at which I ended.

As a child I was sexually assaulted and sexualised by young men who wore uniforms. It is difficult to remember and harder to forget. But this book is the opening of that hotel room door. This book is a run along a well-lit corridor. It is a parent with an open arm and a simple belief in me, as human, as here, as worthwhile. It is all the things that did not happen.

I was a sun-filled child until I reached adolescence, and then everything broke. The pavements shattered around me, the wallpaper stripped, the trees ran away from me, the sky hung low and breathed down my neck. Many reading this will recognise the symptoms of post traumatic shock disorder – the anxiety, the constant feeling of loss, the darkness, the inability to speak, to think, to love, to earn money, to dress, to wash, to smile, to sit to sit to sit. I was continually moving, trying to break free from the skin that had imprisoned me by birth as a woman. I could have been forgiven for believing that I was transgender. But I am not. I am a woman who is afraid of being a woman, and that is very different.

My personal story includes mental health issues, psychiatric hospital, suicide attempts, a repetitive eating disorder, drug addiction, and one fuck of a lot of dancing. Some of the poems within this book reflect that experience, from the moment of apocalypse toward healing, recovery and revolution.

But inside every poem is a poem, and inside that there is another one still. The same principle applies to this book. Once I had begun to see myself, I could not help noticing what was happening to women worldwide. Whilst some of the poems are character based or tell stories of individuals[1], they are not based on any living woman, but every living woman; a composite. I tried to develop a technique when writing that I thought of as 'investigative poetry' much like investigative journalism. This book is what you might get if you crossed a poet with a photo journalist and broke their camera. It's a restless collection that travels in both space and time.

To help me create the collection I have worked with two of the strongest and most vital editors working in poetry today: Sabrina Mahfouz and Anthony Anaxagorou. They each provided critical support to the project at different stages: Anthony commissioning me in the first place, as well as giving forensic advice on editing; and Sabrina as the Content Editor. All of these poems came from phone conversations with them, hungover meetings in Covent Garden cafes, and endless train journeys. All of these poems came from the fact that they were both listening, and I will never be able to thank them adequately.

I have tried to explore different forms throughout the writing, some of which have worked while many other attempts failed. A number of the poems are made up of report cards, or are news headlines or government forms or internet arranged-marriage profiles. It's why some of the poems are character based and in the first person, whilst others are written miles above, shot from the nose of a drone.

There are three sections to the book: Songs of Silence, Songs of Survival and Songs of Uprising. Each section is written to represent a stage in our recovery both as individual women and as universal symbol. Think of it as a symphony in three movements. Think of it as revolution.

[1] With the exception of 'commander pigeon' and 'my father, the lord of war' which are poems based on fictionalised real lives

The writing of this has taken me across the world without leaving my desk. The research process involved reading, interviews, films and conversations. I also led a series of masterclasses across the UK in the period of writing to enable other women to write and own their stories too. The poetry produced in those workshops can be found online in a developing archive of women's voices at www.joelletaylor.co.uk. None of the women's stories from those workshops appear in here, apart from the section of Landays, written by Afghan women refugees from Paiwand. In that section the women write in the poetic form of Landay (short, poisonous snake) about their lives and their losses using the old folk form of chant. It is an act of some rebellion in Taliban controlled Afghanistan for any woman to write, and some have been executed for what amounts to poetry. It seemed to me that the only people entitled to write in that form, rich with blood and loss and longing, were the forbidden poets themselves, the women refugees from Afghanistan. You can read more about them further on in this book and on my website.

Toward the end of the collection I have added a list of references, both personal and academic, listing my sources.

No book that attempts to write about the experiences of women worldwide could even begin without serious discussion and thought around ideas of appropriation, and what it means semantically speaking for a white working class woman living in a privileged world to write about those women of colour worldwide who do not have my privilege of relative safety, access to education, and ultimately opportunities to publish.

Please consider these poems news reports – poetry reportage – and help me work toward increasing access to publishing for all women, so that all stories have the prospect of being told directly. An attempt to redress this imbalance in opportunity and access to the arts has been made with a masterclass tour of the UK focussing on marginalised communities of women, generously funded by the Arts Council, and also in the commissioning and paying of women to contribute to the Landay section of the book. Small steps, but they all face forward.

What can be certain from my studies is that misogyny is prevalent in every country on the planet, no matter the dominant political ideologies or faiths. All of the major religions are misogynist in nature, blaming the separation of Man from God on the fall of Woman. Whilst some regimes are more brutal, leading to mass murders of women – both adult and unborn – others are more insidious; the recent removal of reproductive rights from women in America, and the abortion laws in Ireland.

As I write this 3,537 Yazidi women have been kidnapped with at least a third being sold in chains by Daesh; five queer women were beaten outside a UK pub in a misogynist homophobic attack; you can buy a pretty Asian bride over the internet (you can buy girl children there too. The starting price is around $300); in every war recorded 'enemy' women are either deported to rape camps or their routine sexual violation is seen as one of the inevitable consequences of war. In short, women are a weapon of war, used as a means of demoralising the male soldiers of opposing sides. Women are abducted and forced to marry strangers in several countries, prominent among them Pakistan and Kyrgyzstan; in China selective abortions have decimated the female population, leading many men to turn to Vietnam to find partners. Most buy them. Elsewhere, New Delhi is declared the 'Rape Capital of the World' and lower caste girls are sexually violated and hung from trees outside villages in India; meanwhile the corrective rape of lesbians in South Africa has reached epidemic proportions. Females are prevented from accessing education in over 20 countries, leading to illiteracy for around 110 million children, 60 per cent of whom are girls, which in turn leads to lower job prospects, which in turn culminates in limited resources which in the end spells early death. Vital services essential to women are being cut still further in the UK, including domestic violence refuges and rape crisis lines. Benefits for working women are slashed.

Childcare provision is limited. In some of our treasured Western democracies women no longer have the right to freedom over their own bodies, their reproductive rights removed by the democratic decision of white men. The UK Conservative party has announced a coalition government with the DUP, a Northern Irish right wing party that believes LGBTQI rights should be abolished and women should not have control over their reproductive rights.

This is a book about that colonisation and terrorism, about invasion and ownership. It is a survival manual, a map, a photograph, a song. It is internet at 2am. It is the way your mother just looked at you. It is the way the girl in front of you on the soft journey home just reached for her keys. This book is your hand reaching for keys.

Joelle Taylor
May 2017

Foreword

Joelle Taylor is a writer whose words get me fired up before they even get to the 'real writing' part of it. The introductions, the notes, the titles to her work take me immediately to a place I have spent days living in and years escaping from. I know a huge number of people who feel the same way and turn to Joelle's work when there is an urge to remember that there's positives to be found cemented amongst the paving slabs of pain – even if these positives are only that there is solidarity, that you are not alone.

The beauty of the poetry in *Songs My Enemy Taught Me* is so extraordinary, that this too becomes a positive, becomes a peg to keep yourself steady but blowing around with incongruous excitement as you read about 'those whose smiles are snapped washing lines' and of 'a mother who hangs a string of bullets around her neck'. Women who are exceptional and exceptionally ordinary. They are the everyday and the everywoman and they are suffering, yes, but they are never defeated and the war imagery that runs explicitly and implicitly throughout this book doesn't let you forget that for a moment. Women across the globe are engaged in a perennial battle – for autonomy over their bodies, for education, for equal opportunities, for a life free from violence, coercion and manipulation. Even the Scandinavian countries lauded as the most gender equal in the world are home to women having to fight against at least some of these oppressions, be it in the public or private realm. Countries that are engaged in armed battle with other states or with domestic factions are home to women facing a daily struggle for basic survival, but the other battles remain to make their lives even more onerous.

Joelle has worked with a remarkable number of women from such a wide range of backgrounds and with such unique experiences, that it is heartening to feel the absolute thread of solidarity that runs through the contemporary struggles examined in this book, whilst acknowledging that each struggle is specific and weighed down with its own history of racist, homophobic, ableist, transphobic, Islamophobic, anti-semitic, whorephobic, xenophobic misogyny.

The bravery of sharing her own traumatic experience as a child has in no way held Joelle back in her ingenious use of experimental form and highly metaphorical imagery. If anything, it has strengthened every word, imbued as the reader knows it is with the skin, sky, sun, clothes, smiles and butterflies that have helped hold the writer together over the years and will no doubt now do the same for countless others.

A quote from the poem 'Colony' stays with me as an image of both exploitation and empowerment that this book encapsulates so movingly and powerfully:

'the emperor is wearing clothes, daughter and they are yours.'

I hope you feel ready to join the universal fight for all daughters to get those clothes back after reading this startling and stunning book.

Sabrina Mahfouz

'Make it political as hell. Make it irrevocably beautiful.'

—Toni Morrison

for Ann Hurley and Kathleen Seary
and for all our mothers

SONGS
OF
SILENCE

Silence was a song my enemy taught me

Canto

(i)

I carry the war in my womb.

At night it kicks
and sings stories of the
first night that war came calling.

Blackpool.
1973.

Small. We are refugees of the economic crisis that has cut power lines and muted the mouths of coal mines and left uroborus dole queues flailing in its wake.

The seaside hotel flung open its doors for us, and flapped its window sashes, as we arrived to make camp for the winter. Songs were written about us.

We pitched our tents in the living room. It was Christmas. Strangers ballroom-danced around us.

At midnight we dug ourselves into our muddy beds. Everybody slept.
I stayed on watch. I am still on watch.

When the war came I was eating vol-au-vents from a paper plate. When the war came I was forcing my Sindy doll into a shapeless Eagle Eye action man uniform. When the war came I was sellotaping a rifle to the frozen hand of my Barbie.

When the war came it was gentle. When the war came it was singing. The scent of war is Old Spice, is lager, is late night take away. The sound of war is silence. Is a small girl with a mouth as wide as a coal mine that eats the whole town. In the morning there were boot marks across the board games.

(ii)

The bed is cold and my teeth are abandoned buildings
and somewhere there is the smell of something burning
a book. a flag. a letter.
In my room at the top of the seaside hotel
there is a single bed with a white sheet.
I cannot think of anything to write on it.
The bed is a slowly developing photograph:

Here's us around the dinner table
we are smiling like carved meat;
no one notices that the daughter is eating herself.

Here's you walking home from school
your shadow walks behind you as if ashamed
even the trees whisper about you
you have embarrassed the wind.

Here's him. And him. And him.
A family portrait. Successful. Ironing their uniforms and double-folding their smiles
catching children delivered from the conveyor belt of their wives' wombs
and holding them up to the bare lightbulb to bless.
It's okay. They are boys.

Here are the stairs
and here, the long corridor you are afraid to walk along
perhaps it is your cervix.
It is your cervix.

(iii)

My womb is a war zone after everything is taken.
After the soldiers have left
spitting into the palms of their hands

after the shelves have been emptied and only sell nothing

after the nothing gathers in great mountains at the sides of the streets
after the streets are running with hungry ghosts
after women's skins are slung from washing lines
after children write their names in the dust that was once their fathers

I carry the war in my womb.
Perhaps this is what happened:
someone said my hymen was a door behind which rebels were making plans
and they kicked it in
paced the room and filled their pockets with valuables
my mother's wedding ring. my first tooth. a bright blue hair bobble. your address. this.
They wanted to know where I was hidden.
I wanted to know where I was hidden.
I am the corner of the room
I am a crime scene
an invaded land
an oil rich country
I will be divided equally between nations.

(iv)

12 years old. There are small bodies washed up on the shores of my eyes.
When my photograph is taken another girl's face appears instead of mine.

(v)

There are men seated quietly at municipal Formica desks at the neck of my womb.
'You do not look like your photograph' they say *'please state the purpose of your visit'*
'Did you pack these bags yourself?'
My sandbag hips.
My barbed wire hill.
Many will die defending it,
others will drown in the sediment of a trench whose walls are always caving in.

My cunt is a bomb crater the villagers gather around the edge of and peer into. Sometimes smoke rises from deep within. These are my ghosts. These are messages in a lost language. Capture them in jars. Display them on suburban mantelpieces. In memes. On t-shirts. Smile. Be my friendly enemy.

(vi)

When you are impregnated by war you give birth to bullets. Name them. Show them his scent.

The palm of my small right hand is a creased map to safety. I am stopped at the border. I cannot remember my name in your language.

My skin is a white flag

I am waving now. I am holding my skin above my head.

Stop shooting. Stop shooting. Stop shouting. War is an unexploded kiss, buried. The battleground is the bedroom in which two people stand in opposing trenches behind sandbag pillows saying I Love You wrong. That's not how you say it. *This is how you say it.*

My skin is partitioned.
This bit is yours.
Parts of my body speak different languages;
after the war I was colonised.
Use my blood to power your generators
dig deep in me for your gemstones
harvest my hair and eyelashes, these
drips of words on my chin.
And you:
you I give my womb to.
Feed it well. Walk it when needed.
Listen at night to its curling song.

(vii)

the girl whose eyes are shallow graves beneath suburban patios goes to school and rows of heavy wooden lidded desks are filled with the smiling dead. When the world ended nobody noticed. The sun has eaten itself. Skeleton birds mutter bone songs.

Her mother and father tell jokes about her
everybody laughs
the girl whose eyes are fox holes laughs
the teacher laughs
children gathered like litter around the stairwell laugh
the social worker laughs
the policeman laughs
the doctor laughs
the psychiatrist giggles
the world ends.

(viii)

I remember how silence was a choir.

There's you in the kitchen, vibrato.
There's you at the back of the class, soprano.
There's you walking home, tenor:
your solo silences are everywhere.

(ix)

This is not what I meant to say.
I once witnessed my own murder. It was Wednesday. It is always Wednesday.

After my death people continued talking to me as though I were still there.
After my death people tried to hold me but their hands passed through my skin.

After my death I came back to haunt myself, often
catching glimpses of my ghost sitting in the same chair as me, speaking
through my mouth, ahead of me in
the dinner queue
my bright blue bobble dancing just out of reach in a crowd, an
ankle disappearing around a corner.

(x)

When war was teething it rubbed its soft teeth against pavements and
trees and wallpaper and lovers. It refused to let go of my hand in public. I
lost sight of war once in the park and its screams were sirens and the wail
of bombs. I hit people I love, my bombing is imprecise. This is common.
This is to be expected.

(xi)

in the hospital she lies in bed –
she has always lied in bed –
they ask her questions and she focuses on the spelling of the answers;
she is afraid she will not get them right. She cannot get them right.
The true answer is the wrong answer.

(xii)

They show her children who do want to die. They are friendly. One
offers food that she knows will eat her.
She is shown a photograph of an ugly overdose.
She is shown obituaries etched in fingernails.
In his pockets the man with the papercut mouth has a box
it too is small. It too is velvet.
Inside the box mounted at the centre is a large tear, collected a
drip at a time from all of the children under his care. Tears are
crystal balls.
'If you look closely at it, you can see your future' he says
She leans close.
She sees nothing.

(xiii)

When the talking begins the villagers hide in cellars or run in the shade of trees to the other side of the hill. The girl with the dugout eyes watches them leave and stops speaking. She talks to a piece of paper in her hand instead. People queue up to look at it. There are so many peering over her shoulder that she has to stand on the hill and read it out to everyone. They clap. They look pleased. She forgets what she is saying.

(xiv)

For Christmas I give my mother an uncomfortable truth.
She wears it when I visit.

(xv)

At the core of every woman is the womb.
The bright angry pearl formed of grit and lies and courage and unreturned phone calls and regret rubbed for centuries against one another.
They come to prise it out;
it is a summer morning.
When she awakens she is surrounded by strangers
stranded on islands of tight white beds –
archipelagos strewn across the ward –
she waves
but every stranded woman is waving to someone else
who is waving to someone else;
ships pass and do not see them

(xvi)

Later I am dressed in bunting and songs are composed to keep my spirits up. Later we are given ration books of kisses, three hand-holdings a month. One dry night. There is never enough to go around. Grown men on street corners cower and wonder at the cracks cobwebbing their faces, not knowing they are smiles.

(xvii)

After the war there was singing. After the war there were ceremonies of remembrance. We remember the living, and finally carve our own names into our gravestone teeth. After the war we set out to find the others and guide them home. We lit fires in our windows and tapped Morse over screwed rubble. Some rubble tapped back.
Some rubble grew hands and we pulled on them until we had uprooted a forest of women, shaking their heads of soil, of shame, and brushing silence from their shoulders. Thank you, they said. Thank you.

We have been waiting.

flirting with death

women's refuge, 2014

(i)

There wasn't much eye contact if I'm honest or
gentle collusion of knees, the
electricity of restraint or
grass growing through flagstone tongues
he was behind me
most of the way –
I think I knew he was behind me years before he was
He has always been behind me, I thought;
his step matching the tide of my shadow
his breath thick with escaping birds.
It is in moments like these, I thought, that I
wish that the clutched keys could
open air itself,
that I could step in, that I could
crawl back inside
the Everything;
that I could zip the air up
in a thin vertical line
behind me.

(ii)

Look. This isn't what I meant to say.
Cigarette?
The fact is that I knew he was dangerous the first time
his eyes walked my body
like a building inspector looking for weaknesses in the architecture
and let me tell you

I knew then I'd need to wear a hard hat around him;
But you know
we all love a bit of danger, don't we?
We all love bit of blood and glamour.

A bit of spit and sour.
It's what keeps us alive, isn't it?
This sense of near-death?
That's what love is.

I've been walking on eggshells for years, love.
Never broken one.

(iii)

You don't know him like I know him
that's what makes it so hard
knowing him, that is.
If I didn't know him,
if he was a headline, say
then I'd know what to do
I would. I would know.

You don't see him when he is crying.
You don't see him when he's a small boy abandoned by a bedroom door,
listening to his heart beat hard on the other side.
You don't see him when he is a small boy falling from the side of a mountain.

my father, the lord of war[2]

Bosnia, 1992

There is a tiger at the dinner table.
He holds his cutlery neatly between thick paws
and wipes steak red lips on the table cloth
each of his amber eyes an exit wound.
He makes gentle conversation
light bounces off silver;
the tiger at the dinner table
is a creature of culture, of vandalism.
He wears the bars across his chest to remind him of the
camp at Omarska
and the long Winter. Do you remember it? The laughter around the
mess hall table. The willingness of women.

Sometimes the tiger sings.
He throws back his throat
and out of his mouth climb
the 250 of Vukovar
Some dragging saline drips, others clutching stethoscopes like
crucifixes
And here is a woman, alone,
peering through shell-damaged buildings
of teeth,
and now a football team
sung onto the dinner table.

I keep my eyes down and eat.

The tiger at the dinner table knows what I will be wearing
for school tomorrow.

[2] This is a poem about living with a War Lord, and full information on Arkan (in this case) is provided within the Reference section of the book.

He knows the name of the boy I will smile once at.
He knows how my mother breathes,
and why.

The tiger keeps a white eagle in a gilded cage on the mantelpiece.
It reminds him of home. He feeds it small things without names.

The hunters crowd the windows
to watch the tiger at my dinner table
but he is clever.
he slips in between the bars on his fur
and makes good his escape
again. There will always be a tiger at the dinner table.

At night he prowls the cement savannahs of suburban Serbia.
From my silent bed
I hear him growl white in the distance
The echo of mumbled artillery

His roar,
Srebrenica.

skin cells[3]

HMP Downview, April 2017

The first prison is the body, Benzo says, and
she is a political prisoner
33 years and no parole,
you get less for murder, she says
at least then you would get privileges,
time off for interesting behaviour,
we are enhanced,
a clockwise walk to wind up the day
the grey dream of leaving.

The first prison is the body, and curled in a corner
is a girl who once looked like me, Benzo says:
I was born inside looking out,
tapping my tin cup against the bars of my ribs
we are born caged
marking off the days with these
thin red lines against skin cells,
digging tunnels with fingernails into soft plaster.

we were once here. and here.

They have removed all sharp objects
these teeth
and her shoes are untied
my feet are free, Benzo says;
she has turned all of the mirrors to face the walls
she once almost fell in a full length one and drowned
but now they only reflect the walls, the infinity of indifference
and the strange thing is, Benzo says
when I have done my time

[3] Please see notes in Reference section of this book for a fuller understanding of the issues affecting women in the prison system.

when the magistrate of my heart finally discharges
it is not called Release Day but
                    Due Date
as though I have been gestating all these years.
Perhaps inside every woman
is another woman.

visitors gather, eat popcorn and stare

We sit with our hands unmoving
mouthing through smeared air at one another
unsure of who is the animal.

first they separate the men from the women

Cambodia, April 1975

We stand in lists at the edges of cities, faces pouring forward into
fields: we wraiths of women who search for our bodies, our last words
evaporating in the width of the heat, to rise above us in low clouds;
there will be a monsoon of women this Spring.

Some of us taken into the earth, seeds tilled into graves; some on
doorsteps refusing to move, squall baby at breast; some at the altar
of mass marriage; or in the bedroom, eyes turned toward the wall;
others still in the long lines leading out from the city, the queue to
enter our new lives;

we are spilled water.

They came for us as the sun spoke our names, while we were
shopping or cooking breakfast, pinning out the laundry or cycling
to work.

Those with soft hands those whose hands are broken birds those
whose hair grows in the dark whose smiles are ingrown those who
wear spectacles what is it that they need to see? those who have white
bars across their noses blistered third fingers those who heal those
who study those whose faces are forbidden texts who think those
whose shoes are unclean those whose heels are typewriters those with
unfitting shirts those whose skirts are whispers those whose eyes are
insults those who dress in disobedience those who pray those who
question those who answer those who marry themselves those with
babies those with an eclipse as their womb those whose kisses are
escaping swarms of night butterflies those who are old those who
are young those whose eyes are escape tunnels those whose faces are
quiet corners those who speak in dead tongues those whose laughter
is muddy is quicksand those who farm minds not fields those who run
those who remain those who eat alone those who sleep alone those
who dream alone those who look to the east those who blink to the
west those whose mouths carry hurricanes those whose silence is an

uprising volcanic chatter those who sit who walk those whose smiles
are snapped washing lines.

The fruit from the killing fields has deep roots and flesh the taste
of surprise.

pub street[4]

Siem Reap, Cambodia, January 2016

EXTERIOR VIEW. CAMERA PANS A STREET LINED WITH BARS AND RESTAURANTS AIMED AT WESTERNERS. THE BARS SPILL ON TO THE STREETS. FLOCKS OF CHILDREN PECK AT TOURISTS. GIRL CHILDREN AND WOMEN ARE DRESSED IN RED. THEY SPEAK RESPECTFULLY TO MEN DRUNK ON MASCULINITY. CAMERA ENTERS BAR. STOPS AT TABLE OF MEN. THEY ARE OF DIFFERENT AGES AND WEAR SIMPLE SHORTS AND T-SHIRTS WITH GLOBAL LABELS.

TO CAMERA:

(i) Andy. Capricorn.

I found her on eBay or Amazon/ can't quite remember/ not Argos though/ I had been looking for a while/ long sticky nights alone/ down there in the basement/ too cold/ scrolling faces/ as though I could swipe each expression/ click and find out more/ If only more women were like this/ I thought/ that we could click and know/ she speaks English/ basic/ but what words does she need/ only yes/ and when, perhaps/ my feeling is that sometimes words are used to prevent communication/ is that a cliché?/ who is watching this?/ her name is difficult to say in my language/ so I just call her Girl.

She likes it.

(ii) Steve. Leo.

Basically/ like any decent man I'm just looking for love/ after my wife left/ slammed the door of her bitter little heart/ didn't she/ and turned all the kids against me/ whispering while they were sleeping/ didn't she/ after that I just thought/ fuck it/ and sold up/ and came

[4] Please see notes in Reference section for a fuller understanding of the sex tourism industry in Cambodia and South East Asia.

here/ you can do anything here/ no rules/ not in the same way/ and the girls wear red/ which makes it easier somehow/ for both of us/ yes/ I think now finally/ after 50 long years walking this road/ I have finally found paradise.

Yes. That really is her name.

(iii) Alexander. Cancer.

What people don't understand/ is that they like it/ I'm gentle you know/ most of us are/ there are one or two bad ones of course/ but this is love/ I express love for the girl/ in a way which helps her to grow/ into a beautiful woman/ I help her to understand her own body/ like a guide/ no/ think of me as a tourist/ and she is Cambodia/ I wander through the side streets and alleyways/ through the temples and markets/ the shanty stalls and insect stands/ and translate her body/ into mine.

(iv) Chris. Scorpio.

You don't just marry the girl/ you know/ you marry the whole country/ you join lands/ it's like a colonisation/ I sometimes think/ in a nice way/ we have moved into their bodies/ quietly at first/ and now in packs of howling men/ and they all come/ all of them/ stand at the side of the street/ and sniff/ you can actually see them sniff/ but I think of Pub Street as a river/ this is Rita/ also known as Nguyen/ we've been married since I first came/ she cooks for me/ you know/ makes good the bed/ all of that/ I like to think I taught her to be human/ that I gave her language/ and fire/ and schools/ a little bit of extra cash for the side days.

I come out here to fish. It's easy. All you need is a rod and a hook, and they practically swim into the pan.

fuck you's[5]

Dark Web, 2017

14 years. Virgin.
Basic English. Communist.
The Great Leap Forward.

western union bitcoin
three thousand for this child, cheap
add to hot list.

catalogue of girls
batteries not included
flat pack assembly.

[5] A cut up poem taken from text used in sex trafficking or buy-a-bride websites. See Reference section.

event horizon[6]

West Africa, 2017

$3 for this cut this termination this event horizon this hyphen
into female
this underline of sex
this —
this exorcism
this hole within a hole;
this whole cut is worth more than
my daughter or hers or
the white crow who pecks at the skirts of children gathered in swarms
beside the hut
This cut
is a flag, a cultural revolution. Maimouna washes her hands in the
back room, some say in the tears of mothers, some say in her own,
some do not speak at all.
But we the women know
this is her black hole, that will eat
her whole,
repelling fully grown men in orbit around her thighs;
she has eaten the universe this
girl child
this soft lip stupid,
she is a worm hole
and no one can remember where she leads.

She wonders if they will speak the same language at the other end of
the black hole. After this: nothing else.

the imam tells them that the thing they remove

[6] Please see Reference section for information regarding female genital mutilation.

is itchy
so itchy that girls take wire scrubbers to themselves
so itchy that it is enflamed, a volcano, unsure footing
so itchy
that a girl might be tempted to ease the itching one day
might rub rub rub herself into water
and little else.
This is the fate of girls.

cut out the itch.
It is a pretty thing.

The best of men wear them mounted on rings or
dangling from forested necks at moon break.

marching song for Leshia Evans[7]
USA, 2016

this white is a uniform we cannot remove;
slip out of at the end of a breathless night
where the stars are exit wounds in black skin
and the air is haunted by eagles circling.
we cannot walk these uniforms on the slow heel toe
behind black coffins laden with absence
we cannot leave it folded in anthems at the end of the bed;
it follows us into our dreams, sister
where our skin is a flag across our chests,
we are powerful now.
the smallest of us are powerful now.

white skin is a uniform you cannot remove, comrade
and the stains will not come out; I have tried
to scrub this blood pigment that spreads into a map of Ferguson
of Tottenham
of Cairo of Moscow Warsaw Berlin.
you will flinch unconsciously as we walk into the room, sister, and
pretend it is white fly. It is white fly.
our skin so white it is invisible to us:

we were skinless at Greenham, skinless in Molesworth, we were
skinless at Yarrow, skinless in Nottingham, skinless on the picket line,
skinless at the coal mine, we were skinless against the war, skinless
against taxing the poor, skinless against benefit cuts —

we marched skinless to the song of our feet
all one

white skin could not see we were wearing the enemy
skin so white it was invisible to us.
but when they came
bluebottles with badges and grins torn from newspaper front pages

[7] Please go to notes in Reference section.

white skin smiled at policeman
white skin apologised to court
white skin went home with a warning
white skin went to sleep in white sheets in a white room in a white house
on the white side of town
woke to a white sky

did you not get the memo, sister?
(It was written in white ink on white paper)
we were white-teous
so white-teous

our shadows are in awe of us, but
white skin is silence, is white noise
our borders are portable;
white skin is
confetti at a funeral;
they say the flames from the car were white hot
and children played in the ashes;
it lay in white folds across their faces.

white skin is a uniform
a torn placard
a coward's retreat
a rolled back eye,
the grit of guards' teeth
an unwritten letter home
a petition. shared and shared again.
an unstamped passport

a lost birth certificate
the white cliffs of Dover
white skin is the chalk outline around her body

a shroud

homs sweet homs[8]

Syria, Spring 2015

Women live among the rubble
hanging washing from the limbs of buildings
and the lines of the hungry,
waiting for question marks of men to return.

The children have stopped crying now. Infant shrieks left in the beaks of birds. Tears have migrated faces. Mothers war with their reflections in bullet casings. She dances with dust. Can still feel his arm around her waist. She sweeps him up and holds him against her heart. Eagles circle. A bear hammers.

She has repainted the fractured skin of her home and
applied lipstick to the shattered door frame, she has
re-styled the roof, and
shadowed the windows in blue and
carefully positioned the smashed frames of family members in prominent places;
It is only right that the missing wait too.

An old woman collects broken ornaments to piece together again
her face a smashed vase
as she picks quietly through the goods of her children for
that which may be saved.Planted.

Somewhere
a woman burns her dress in the back yard
a mother hangs a string of bullets around her neck
a girl plays house in a deserted city
performing voices of the gone

the songs of silence.

[8] Please see Reference section for statistics regarding female refugees, and internally displaced persons.

god is an atheist[9]

USA, December 2016

Outside, the street eats itself, tail first, swallowing night butterflies, men with paper faces and shouts for eyes, whose fingers invade bottle tops, that chime, sing against their thighs. outside the birds have forgotten the words to their songs and children have taken to ironing their voices before morning assembly. women march backward, and there is a line around everything, even the men, even this —

and all are joined to praise the One True God.

All hail the One True God, who climbed upward on a ladder of lies, who colonised Heaven and built a fast food restaurant, a bookie, a pound shop, astride a throne of Sunday papers, the One True God, whose eyes are Soho neon, whose prayers are cash registers in churches of self-immolating shopping arcades, from congregations of bullet-head boys, gathered on pews of slack-jaw televisions; all hail the One True God, all hail the White, all hail the fat of words, the rind of a man, all hail the rise of his golden skyscraper, his extended middle finger, his bedroom monolith.

They came for Her on a Sunday in the surprise of her summer garden, by the lake, across from the border, silent at first, gathering in swarms; silence is made of everything we forgot to say. The Old God was evicted years ago, pushed over the lip of paradise by a man with a smile like a drunken halo, and now she sits – breathing – a woman with passport stamp eyes and a robe of torn visas; the Old God is held, brown fingers worrying the beads of a chain, in an airport detention centre somewhere left of Chicago, and now the Old God has stopped believing in herself and instead watches the sky for eagles.

[9] Religion and misogyny are close friends. Please go to Reference section for a fuller description of the relationship.

letters home[10]

Vietnam – China, 2017

Dear Má,
Each morning, when the sun is the Chinese flag, the men bring in the young pigs, the cigarette pigs, who scream before they know why; and sometimes I hear the men laugh – though it is the laugh of a plane taking off without you – as they corner a pig and take their time with her. I was in the backroom during the slaughter. I was getting everything ready in the kitchen.
Your daughter Le, with good wishes.

Dear Má,
When I woke up I didn't know I was in China. This is important. I didn't know I was coming, Má. I met him online, just a friend. We chatted for weeks and when we met it was not just him but a whole group of friends. We ate dinner. I remember laughing. We drank alcohol. But I felt tired. Very tired. And when I awoke I was here. Please find me Má.
Your loving daughter, Hwa

Dear Má,
I am married now. I am sorry you could not come to the wedding. I was also absent except in body. My husband is a kind man. I do not know who he is. I want to come home now.
My love always, Hang x

Dear Má,
When they need to make a kill they separate the herd, they select the smallest first and lead her away from the others, with promises and work in far off places, and even love.
Your daughter, Sang

Dear Má,
There are many girls. All of us working. All of us writing these secret messages into the backs of men. They think that they are powerful,

[10] To understand the context of this poem please go to Reference notes.

but it is us who have the power. We have written a thousand letters on these men, and as they spit and leave the room they take our words with them. All men are letters. Read their backs, Má. Read them.
Your child, Thi xxx

Dear Má,
this is a strange restaurant. every meal is the same. the men queue up and we lay on tables.
With love and dreams for our future, you loving daughter, Ai xx

Dear Má,
I auditioned for this. I walked up and down, I smiled. They said it was for customer service on the hotel. But it wasn't. It was to see how well I obeyed orders. I got the job. God Bless America.
the best of me, Phuoc

Dear Má,
Xi has been here for three years now, and still only 16 but she dreams of singing herself into a new body when all of this is done. When she is folded and placed at the end of a bed. When she is posted into herself one last time. I remember the river. I dream of the mosquito. I understand why the cow gives its blood willingly, what it wants to leave. The cow is afraid of its own body.
love Anh x

Dear Má,
They say here that the vagina is a grave that living men are buried in, and if you hold your ear to it you can hear his ghost coming to take you home.
When will his ghost guide me home?
With all good wishes on your year, your faithful daughter,
Phuong xxx

Dear Má,
I am not here.
I am not here still.
I am not
I.

wedding present

West Africa, 2017

She was opened on her wedding day,
a gift from the female line of the family
wrapped in tabloid paper and bound in ribbons of rosary
at birth.

the whole family gathered to watch the unravelling. they ate sandwiches.
some drank. others did not.

her husband tore the paper apart

and took from her
her inheritance.

eulogy for the walking

Ireland, 2013

what shall we do now with our dead children?

make t-shirts from the skin of their faces
shroud them in petitions
knit wreaths from newspaper obituaries
forge flag poles from their bones.

What shall we do now with our dead children?

bury them
like everything else.

360[11]

The World, April 2017

FEMALE TAX

'Girls from low income families are skipping school during their periods because they cannot afford sanitary protection. Charity Freedom4Girls, which normally provides sanitary pads to African school girls, was contacted after teachers in Leeds studied habitual truants and found their monthly absences were down to lack of sanitary protection.' *Metro, 13 March 2017*

SELF MURDER

LaVena Lynn Johnson (July 27, 1985 – July 19, 2005) was a Private First Class in the United States Army whose death, officially ruled a suicide, has attracted international attention amid allegations that her death was the result of rape and murder.

'she was found in her tent with a gunshot wound to her head, a broken nose, black eye, loose teeth, acid burns on her genitals, and a trail of blood leading away from her tent.' The Department of Defence has officially ruled her death a suicide.

UNITED NATIONS OF PAEDOPHILIA

The United Nations is turning a blind eye to child rape within its own ranks. *Andrew MacLeod, 25 March 2017*

INDIAN ACID ATTACKS

Women make up 80 per cent of acid victims, according to Asfi, which says the number of assaults are on the rise. Reasons for attacks include revenge for a refused marriage proposal, family or land disputes, domestic violence or suspicion of infidelity.
Indian government statistics show there were 249 attacks recorded

[11]Explanation in Reference section.

in 2015, a rise of 11 per cent on the previous year. Under-reporting means the figures disguise the true scale of the problem, according to the Human Rights Law Network – an India-based non-profit legal aid organisation – which estimates there at least 1,000 cases per year. *Guardian, April 14 2017*

EQUALITY

'In the latest series of University Challenge, only 22 per cent of competitors were female.' *Guardian, 14 April 2017*

EQUALITY SELFIE

'When medical student Emma Johnson went onto University Challenge, as part of Oxford University's Corpus Christi team, she had no idea she would end up as an internet sensation. Yet after her appearance on the BBC quiz show, she found herself labelled 'the perfect woman.'

'Here she tells Radhika Sanghani how it felt:' *Guardian*

USA DMV ENABLING

'Trump's rigorous asylum proposals endanger domestic abuse survivors. Immigration advocates have been doing battle over the fate of women such as Elbia for more than a decade. Arguing that people who are fleeing gender violence ought to qualify for asylum, they have notched critical court victories for victims of female genital mutilation, forced marriage and homophobic violence.'

'Our country is not a battered woman's shelter,' said the right-wing provocateur Ann Coulter on Sean Hannity's radio show. We're not here to take in all the charity cases of the world.' *Guardian online*

THE FEARLESS GIRL

The sculptor behind the 'Charging Bull' statue near Wall Street in New York said on Wednesday that the 'Fearless Girl' sculpture placed in front of his artwork is a violation of his rights, changing its meaning and context.

IDENTITY CHECKS

Stonewall calls for gender-neutral X option for UK passports

LGBT rights group says many transgender people who do not identify as male or female are put off travelling abroad.

UK passports should allow people who do not identify as male or female to define themselves as X, an LGBT rights group has said.

NUANCE

Mike Pence does not eat alone with women other than his wife, which throws a question on whether there can now be women in power or leadership roles in the United States.

HILLARY CLINTON

In her first interview since losing the 2016 election, Hillary Clinton said misogyny had played a role in her election loss.

Clinton 'spends a lot of time wrestling' with the fact that 53 per cent of white women voted for Trump and the impact of her gender on her loss, she said at the Women in the World summit

'Certainly misogyny played a role,' she said.

LOL

White men 'endangered species' in UK boardrooms, says Tesco chairman

ONE IN THREE

The Caribbean has among the highest rates of sexual assault in the world: according to United Nations statistics from 2015, one in three women have experienced sexual or physical violence at least once in their lives. And it is estimated that 14–38 per cent of women have experienced intimate partner violence at least once.

In Jamaica alone over the past few months, at least eight women have been killed by domestic partners, young women have been abducted and assaulted by taxi drivers and another pastor was charged with sex-related crimes on a minor.

Elsewhere in the region, Unicef estimates that in the eastern Caribbean, between 20 and 45 per cent of children have been sexually abused. In Trinidad, between 2005 and 2015, 300 women were murdered by a domestic partner.

TAMBOURINE ARMY

Early one Sunday in January, a group of women arrived at a church in the rolling, green hills of rural Jamaica. They were not there to worship, but to show support for a young victim of sexual abuse: a 15-year-old girl, who had allegedly been raped by the church's pastor a few weeks earlier.

The 14 activists entered the church and sat in silence, but angry words broke out when they were approached by a different pastor; the confrontation culminated with him being struck in the head by a tambourine.

The incident marked the beginnings of the Tambourine Army, a new organization to fight gender-based violence in Jamaica, which this weekend will mark its arrival with a protest in Kingston. In what is believed to be the largest-ever protest against gender-based violence in the region, similar marches will be held in solidarity with another group called #lifeinleggings in Barbados, Trinidad and Tobago, Antigua and Barbuda, Dominica, the Bahamas and Guyana.

GENDERNAUT

Peggy Whitson has broken the record for most days in space by a US astronaut.

Dr Whitson already holds records for the most spacewalks carried out by a woman astronaut and is the first woman to command the International Space Station (ISS) twice.

At 57, she is also the oldest woman to have gone to space.
BBC NewsBeat

INVISIBILITY

UK WH SMITH LGBTQ BOOK PROMOTION includes mainly gay male authors - only 3 lesbian authors, and no transgender. Two of the lesbian authors featured wrote books about the gay male experience, and are American. *24 April 2017*

DARK WEB

Father and friend raped two year old daughter 9 times and broadcast it on the dark web, in a chat room that had 50 members watching the live stream. *RT.com, 27 April 2017*

ROAD TO HOPE

In a way to promote education for girls, Juri, a village in Jharkhand's East Singhbhum district, has recently named a few of its roads after its most educated girls. *IndiaToday, 24 April 2017*

5 SHOCKING THINGS

Arabia gets elected to UN women's rights commission

A country which does not let women study, work, travel or marry without the permission of their male guardian has been elected to the United Nations Commission on the Status of Women. It was in 2016 that women were finally considered as 'mammals' and not 'objects' in Saudi Arabia. From appalling rape laws to the 'men can eat wife's body parts' fatwa, know 5 shocking rulings passed in Saudi Arabia. *India Today*

invisible women[12]

Chechnya, 2017

We were invisible until they came for us;
then we each appeared
materialising in the middle of fields
at bars
across the desk from you
beside conveyor belts
in school corridors, walking, always walking
or wearing your mother's face.

They can always see us
when they want to erase us.

[12] Notes in Reference section.

the old god

Hackney, 2017

(i)
God is a single mother at the top of the tower block
that borders the motorway, by the slip road, over there, her
pushchair loaded with the Small Emperor of Nothing. She
pushes the weight of her dreams forward
through grey-lipped alleyways and cause-and-effect ways of the
council estate,
across grim-eyed wastelands
where plastic bags blossom on the trees of the outstretched dead,
where stripped branches curl into fists
and shake toward Heaven,
and on she pushes, push
over the playground,
where children stand still, push
past the abandoned swing slung across the arms of a crucifix, push
into the line of oncoming cars.

And He. The New God.
who no longer pays maintenance.
who refuses the bloodline. who sings into bone.
who walks calmly toward the dark flashing lights. His pockets freshly
dug graves.
His teeth a bright city skyline.
He who counts teardrops like pennies; He
whose prayers are accompanied by bailiffs;

the New God does not answer his phone
but instead
sweeps the sky clean of mistakes.

rain is what is left of women.

(ii)
The New God is a bastard.
Born of himself. Man-birthed-man, grown
of dusk stalked sheets and the pocket jingles of
angels getting their wings;
and here is one:
Mary, 16, stealer of night skin, facing
the wall in a small back bedroom in Rotherham, counting
the seconds into to a penny jar on the mantelpiece;
here, Lilith, running, always running, picking
snakes from between her legs and eating them —
men have always forgotten their names around her — and here is
Eve,
sewing orchards across bedsheets
bright black mistakes
these seeds of rebellion
from which a world will grow.

(iii)
The Old God has your number, Jesus, Allah, Mr Etcetera, Mr Same
Same Same,
she knows your address
(nice part of town)
and is coming for you —
slow old woman steps,
hosiery like clinging children —
but she is coming
always coming
and when she arrives

there will be birth.

SONGS
OF
SURVIVAL

colony[13]

London, 2017

Today
you are a colony
you are somewhere off the coast of
a land that does not belong to you.
You are an outpost of the
empire of him
detached from your own land mass
an island drifting
towards the edge of the world.

Your children will learn another man's language
will never quite understand everything you say
ask you to repeat
when you whisper tales of your body
that Old Country
and how you used to own everything in it.

You will say:
never let a man build on you, daughter.
Take a photograph of who you are now
and bury it.

You will say:
the Emperor is wearing clothes, daughter
and they are yours.

[13] See Reference section.

the night butterflies[14]

Brixton, 1995

(i) birth

We are born backwards through derelict factory chimneys, clutching umbilical smoke, landing lip first on the conveyor belt of the pavement, gestating our faces, hatching our voices beneath loose jumpers, pinning badges over each breast: this is the breast that bites, this that feeds. we are difference. we are caught between the two lights. everything begins in the ends.

we are women born backwards. we are women born from ourselves. stretched out across linoleum kitchens, suburban carpets, tower block balconies, pushing, pushing,   push.

First, they separate the men from the women and this is easy for most, is a red sea parting, is an uncomfortable hairstyle, but for some the men and women live beneath the same skin, two refugees from warring countries sheltered under the same tarpaulin, and they are difficult to disentangle, to pluck off fingerprints, to designate appropriate areas to. Clothing does not fit. Bodies do not fit. Faces do not fit faces.

Stand over there.

(ii) clothes that fit

Women are pegged out on washing lines across the small Northern town. they are clustered together in pastel colours by size. by wit. by weight. they are pegged by pony tails and blouse lapels, by forehead skin and rictus grin; some of them wave at girls passing far below, the shadow of the women falling across them sometimes, a tide of expectation, the second hand of a helix clock.

[14] Reference — personal history.

She could not reach the washing line, could not pull down the
body that might fit her, and instead stood by, stitching suits from
insults, until she found clothes in the undergrowth, crumpled as
pornography, and tamed them to her skin. Her clothes are alive.
They are dangerous. They are not fed enough.

I dress myself in thick swathes of naked.
I take off my skin.

Here. Have it. Have it all.

(iii) free range face

I took my face out today on the end of a long leash that stretched
all the way back through my mother to my mother's mother. I walked
my face through the airport and it was stopped and asked to spell
its name in a forgotten language did you pack that face yourself,
love? and my face was thirsty, so I walked it into the bar – you know,
the one with the white flag with the red cross, you know: the knife
wounds, the reminder flag, the blood plaster – and my face was
stopped by a gatekeeper asking it difficult mathematics, its place in
the equation, in the x and y, xx yy, if x equals death, then y equals
why? and having drunk the bitter and sour asked for the bathroom
but my face was stopped at a door with a pictogram of a human
with no legs, no agency, mute, the universal symbol for woman,
and my face was asked to declare its country before entering – the
borders to the bathrooms have tightened up their security, too many
insurgents, too many women with landmines beneath their skin,
giving birth to bad dreams in bathrooms, just like this one. and so we
left, my face and I, and I took my face to the club, but it was dressed
too casually, its skin too loose these days, as though it were trying
to find a quiet escape from my face, as though it was an unravelling
rope from a high window, and so I took it took get its hair cut, but the
hairdresser did not understand the slant of the scalp, said the spiral
of crown was anticlockwise, and so I took my face to a field, to a
nothing, a nowhere, where the seeds of women are sown, and there

I set it free.

(iv) how to walk a dog

This is the correct way to comb your hair.
This is the correct way to apply eye liner.
This is this the stick for your lips.
this is the leash for your waist.
this is the muzzle for your breasts.
Fetch.

(v) not raving. drowning.

'It was the end of the world, and it was time to dance.' —Derek Jarman

It is never too late to have a childhood.

Some cocoons are leather, are cocaine; some cocoons are sewn from dark streets at folding time, when all of us origami girls, us bent bois, flutter through club doors in great swarms of badly spelled butterflies, in black and orange, in red and in blue and in black again, in black, in black, with good stitching around the lips; fashion is in the detail, is in the way the whole of the unspoken night is within each of our eyes.

We are incubated in the club light; is it true that lightbulbs attract the dark? we are born onto a stuttering dancefloor, on which I first told you my name, beat it out in Morse code boots; I have been stuck in the same dance step for seventeen years: the dance floor, his face, his grave, my birthing point. I have been dancing for seventeen years, and still no rain, just water. dancing is a form of breathing. we take our closed-down nightclub eyes, and are compelled to dance

forward forward forward.

I remember the morning we looked across the deserted dancefloor at the burning embers of lovers, at the clusters of hands, and the bees. You said you saw a beam of light; that it was the finger of God, and I asked you if that was a new kind of Ecstasy. In a way, you said, in a way.

The bathroom is full of hummingbirds, long beaks crouched over white pollen, limbs cutting the air so quickly that they hardly appeared to move at all, birds flying backwards. I once followed a thin white line out of the club door into a waiting car, which followed a thin white line to a living room in a tower block, and I stayed there for 12 years. lines formed around my mouth and eyes.

(vi) Chill Out

We have bandaged over the windows. the soundtrack is a low hum of everything, and women are displayed in drifts across the bare flat. we sit in ornamental bird cages, pecking at pollen through the bars, dancing on high struts, pulling our feathers out with teeth, as sharp as remarks. here, we are usual. here, we are handsome. we swap feathers and with each feather: a story.

Do you remember that time when Helen danced to the low fi in an all-night supermarket? fuck, love her, thought she was clubbing, daft sod; do you remember when we went to that sex party, thinking there would be drugs, but there were just women eating vol-au-vents in leather hoists; do you remember the long good Friday, rolled notes passed like batons in an increasingly fast relay race

do you remember the grief of day, the eating of infinity?

We wore the night skies beneath our eyes, night butterflies, our wings of leather and torn love letters; do you remember Cass? the empty bar seat, the garlands of garlic on gravestones? do you remember that time we dug a tunnel into Turnmills through the homeless shelter next door;

that time there was no time?

Do you remember any of it?

Me neither.

we are angels with dirty fingernails, skin of cement, goat beards of scrubland; we draw our faces in thick crayon so we can remember where they are; make-up is a map, facial coordinates; I shave my head so that no one can climb up to save me. I peer down at falling boys and see myself in their eyes, a woman disappearing down a well, falling back into myself

ready to be born again. hello Jesus, love. got a light?

(vii) giving birth

a woman sits cross legged on a single bed in Brixton, she has a typewriter between her knees, a skinny grey bird with a swollen belly, pecking at paper, at seeds of words, bent double, so that she is almost uroborus, she is almost eating her own tail. but when she looks down another head is staring back up at her from the space, the parenthesis, the absence of her legs. it is her face. and this time, she recognises it.

she selects a new skin from the wardrobe

and opens the door.

you will give birth many times in a life that is 5 dogs long. you will have many children.

all of the children will be you.

landmines

Accrington, 1982

(i)

How to walk across a woman

Be careful when you walk on me
brother
a small soldier
buried landmines beneath my skin
when I was sleeping
and I cannot remember
where they are buried.
Tread carefully
brother
we are unexploded
we are at the edge of the village
we are waiting outside locked doors
we are in your tourist areas
we are lining the borders
we are your farmed land
we are expanding the boundaries of our bodies
we are insurgent.

(ii)

How to bury a landmine

make it dark
make it still
make it where children walk
make it shallow
make it hidden
make it whisper
make it promises

make it silent
make it wait
make it wait
make it wait.

(iii)

How to navigate a mine field

you will find that all of the maps were destroyed in the last
conflagration. you will find that they were shredded and used to stuff
mattresses, that they were posted to distant lands please keep me safe
where they are used as table mats or drawer linings or gags for rebel
mouths. you will find that all record of the landmines is lost, except
in the shape of unquiet conversation or the murmur of dream, the
pattern of needlework on cloth, on skin

but there is tell of an old one, one who remembers the times of the
burying one who can lead you safely across to the other side

of the girl.

the long grass

Bristol, April 2017

and so it is morning and you are playing.

you must understand that some of this grass is snake. Hear him.
That is snake song.

you must understand that when it comes it is as quick as snake that
snake whisper come here that you go to snake and snake fastens and
snake eat and snake swallow and you are hollow and you are bent
and you are crouching

giving birth to dirt holes.

It is the only way to protect against snakes.

the hole of us[15]

for k.j morris and all the women who look like me
Orlando, 2016

they say

that she loved deep as bullet wounds, that her smile was lightning
and her skin was static; that she was shadow and fire and breath.
Interference. Ignition. Metamorphosis. that her heart was a butterfly
in flame, that broke away from her chest, that pollinated newspaper
ink and back-garden gossip, that perhaps books were written on each
wing, that perhaps years before now her pulse was gunfire disco

that armies are nurtured within women.

But in the machinery of evening, when she looked into the barrel she
saw her father's face – no – she saw a door, blue like the last bruise
he gave her – sorry – a parting gift, her inheritance from a house that
had forgotten her name, on a street where everyone whispered it

and yellow lit a father cutting up a suit in the bedroom.

they say

that she walked like she had war between her legs, like her cunt was
an exit wound, a gun barrel; she walked like she had war between
her legs, a silent dining room in her belly, and that her hair was the
collapse of love, the razing of the town behind her, the men lined at
the sides whistling for wolves, and her breath was a football chant, a
slammed door her laugh was broken glass, her mouth the corner they
first caught her in, her lips the edge of the kerb she hoped would
warp its arms around her, her smile a road she was afraid to walk
along alone, and her speech was

[15] Turn to Reference section for information about K.J. Morris and the Pulse nightclub massacre.

civil unrest, and her skin, a torn shirt, a badly typed hate speech, artex and anaglypta, but she walked like she had war between her legs.

Trigger.

In the eye of the barrel she saw

every back alley stare she kicked aside, every quietened bar, every push from a toilet stall *miss are you man? miss are you a man?* every question every question every, every man with his back turned, every muttered opera of hatred, *every dyke-cunt-queer*, every bitch muzzled, every punch to the nape of the neck – *it was Tuesday, I was just buying tobacco coming home late through Brixton through Istanbul through Berlin through Washington through Kabul* – she saw every bulled night at broken-hearted bus stops, every daggered key, every hard-breath step, every siren of abuse, the circle of night butterflies, the wail of masculinity, the broken chair, the drunken choir of gunfire, the hole.

Aim.

and that hole

was a mouth trying to say its name, was the pin she pushed into the map that led her here to this place of badly drawn women and tan line cartoons, was the centre of the target, was the grave they lowered her into like she lowered herself to meet their gaze, *a door way an alleyway the only way home*, was the hole left in his chest when she left, the unblinking eye of a forgotten god, dad
an embryo.

(They say she played darts, you know
left the board pocked with holes
that she coaxed snooker balls deep into vulvic pockets)

And her father is a hole too. her father is a hole. a chalk line around her heart

We do not speak of him now
but you should know, she carried him in her breast pocket all of these years.

Fire.

they say all women are lowered into our own holes at the end
returned to earth, buried in our own cunts, returned
to female.

they say
that she walked like she had war between her legs
and if you listen closely you can hear the approaching planes.

mary, patron saint of slags[16]

Southern Ireland, 1986

The mother of Jesus was a common whore,
he said, showing his wailing wall teeth
to a class of orbiting eyebrows
she was a slut
a brown harlot
who drank Roman wine
and skin,
who swung her labia in the laybys of the Road to Damascus
filthy whore
who carved stilettos from crucifix
fashioned cleavage from minarets
a common mud sparrow
sky slag
her burkha as tight as
you know
her laugh closing time in Bethlehem
roll up roll up, lads
her rivers polluted with the sputum of love
ordinary men float face down in her;
the mother of Jesus was a common whore.

Strange, he said
how something
so beautiful
so white
can rise from
mud belly

[16] See notes on misogyny and organised religion.

free speech[17]

HMP Holloway, 2014

She stopped writing when the paper stopped listening,
when her handwriting bent too far backward
trying to escape the sentence. The inevitability of it.
An unfocussed page is what silence looks like,
is what an open mouth looks like when
all the words have left, packing bags and family heirlooms, a childhood poster,
to set up home somewhere
kinder.
There is a recklessness about writing sometimes.
More so for these women, forbidden the pen.
The thing about you, Miss, she said, *is that you don't really understand what is inside a pen,*
how ink is homunculus. How there are people inside.
How feint blue bars translate into prison cells;
You think speech is free, Miss,
but it is tagged. Under probation. Free
speech is lining up pennies in a half-way house
in Deptford; free speech
is tearing up voter registration cards, so that he
cannot find her;
she is curled in the centre of a circle of barking bailiffs
they have the scent of her now; free speech
is explaining herself again on Instagram, is walking soft footed across social media bridges
do not wake the troll; free speech
is #*not all men*, is
#white lives matter, is
white noise; free speech
is an empty desk in Juarez, free speech is
missing from lessons this morning
is walking the tightrope of the border between
Mexico and America; free speech

[17] Please see Reference section for notes on the names cited within the poem.

is lined up against a wall in Bulawayo
her hands sprayed blue; free speech is
in indigenous. is found in an alley in Canada, mouth filled with soil;
free speech
is Aziza and Nadia, walking backward from a café in France,
is Sirikan Charoensiri red-eyed in Bangkok gangways
is Tep Vanny, building houses from bones
is Leila De Lima, thrown to the liars, eaten by Duterte,
is Wai Wai Nu, whispering through the bars of her teeth,
is Trần Thị Nga, beaten before her children;

free speech
is expensive around these parts.

it is better to leave it there where you found it, Miss,
on the mantelpiece, in the pretty cage, pecking at the bones of
truth.

men who live beneath bridges. 1.[18]

Traveller Social Media Site, Spring 2017

He says he'll make boxing gloves of her babies and beat her to death with them, he says
she is dust
the edge of the sink the undergrowth, he
says she is dark matter;
everything comes from her,
everything;
the pink seeds that scream night
the way small mouths open wide enough to eat whole lives, dreams, weekend heart-riots
with the boys,
I was going to be someone, he said, but forgot who that was, walked straight past him on my way into her;
in the morning
sheets were stained the shape of nothing much, long car rides, grey roads that
become conveyor belts that feed into the factory, the family factory, that turns as one to eat him.

last night he was powerful
king of the sagging settee, Emperor of Shouts,
noting how like a fist
a baby is.

[18] Please see Reference notes for context in which this poem was created.

men who live beneath bridges. 2.[19]

Liverpool, April 2017

well if she wants to try and punch a full grown man in the face then she shouldn't be surprised if he smacks her one back and yes, I can see that he's bigger and he's a bouncer trained to restrain and all that and yes, I know that she was pissed but that still doesn't make it right does it that she should just try and hit him like that and he does nothing that doesn't make it right feminism you can't have it both ways and what is he supposed to do just stand there and take it just stand there and let this this drunk woman take him down in the street no you have to draw a line there are limits how could he not react he had a split second to decide and in that time in that time he pulled his arm back

all the way to the middle ages
and released his fists
like
caged dogs,

these fists have the scent of women on them, they
will always find her
takes a dog to find a bitch
sniffing through the streets, his fists
pull on their leash
piss on girls
and mark their territory.

[19] Please turn to Reference section for a description of the social media messages that led to this poem.

umbilical

Greenham Common, 1984

we made a rope from our umbilical
from our clothes
our sawn off miniskirts, our blouses of restraint, our nets of tights
our cages of corsets, from
our hair, our false eyelashes, our smiles.

we anchored the rope under the window ledge with one sharpened aside
and jumped.

add to the rope.
everything that binds you is a thread in it
jump
swing into your bodies.

fight club

Lancashire, 1980

My father taught me how to fight
on a rapture Sunday in the living room
of a well-spoken terraced home
somewhere joyful I've forgotten the words to
with a carpet that didn't understand me
and a partition wall he had built himself.

This is how you fall.
This is how you curl a fist into bad grammar.
This is how you hold your breath above your head.
This is how to straighten the skirt of your stomach,
and this:
this is how you smile:

your smile is a magazine of ammunition, a bullet roll
keep it clean. keep it oiled.

Years later
we were caught beating the girl out of her;
out of
ourselves;
we left the girls in us
lain face down on the cement
don't look in the eyes or you'll be trapped there
in blood the colour of uprising
the shape of insolence.

report card

Lancashire, 1977

RE: CLAIRE WILKINSON FORM 8B MS GARDENER
Form Teacher: Claire is doing well in class though does not seem to mix well with the other girls - or boys for that matter. She keeps herself small and quiet. Sometimes it is as though she is not there, as though I can look directly through her to the window and from there to the estates opposite the school, and through there see her family moving around what is left of her home now that everything is broken. I sometimes see her mother looking back at me
Mathematics: Claire is a competent enough mathematician though seems to have difficulty with adding up. Her understanding of fractions is above her age. She understands subtractions too well, and each week there is a little less of her.
Geography: Her teacher tells me that Claire is like Thailand, once beautiful and now built up in primary colours, with strip club eyes and neon lips that flash semaphore at boys in the playground. He tells me that boys visit, but never stay. He tells me that you would not want to live there.
Physical Education: Claire runs as though trying to escape her skin, or breasts or mouth.
Drama: Claire has a flair for the dramatic. She plays herself very well. Other people live in her face.
English: Claire writes. In the classroom I watch her falling into her book, and sometimes wish I could reach out and catch her hand as she slips. She is one of those girls who you are afraid will stumble over the edge of the page.
History: Claire's history is recorded in the rings beneath her eyes. From now on a part of her will always be at her desk in the history lesson, a part of her will always be a small girl wondering what she did wrong.

mass[20]

Magdalene Laundries, Ireland 1944

(i)
Mother Ireland
you cannot wash your women clean or
fold their tongues neatly,
double press the cemetery soil;
bones rise and
point at the sky.

(ii)
I am lighting a candle for Caitlin
for every woman who has been walked through *a ghost*
who haunts her own body,
who lives beneath the burning
bridge of her tongue;
they took her before she could spell No, and
made her body consecrated ground within which
the Fathers could be buried,
and they lie beneath her cemetery skin still,
scratching at coffin lids and spitting
blessings. She eats her own kisses.
How like a church bell a heart is. How like mass.
How like a chain, the rosary.

(iii)
I am lighting a candle for Bernadette
The first thing you must know is
that she is *grateful.*
the second thing
is that she kept her lips
like the nuns said she *should have kept your legs*
she never told of the dark lane the silver eye
shut up

[20] Please see Reference section for an understanding of the Magdalene Laundries in Ireland and the devastating effect they had on generations of Irish women & children.

and now her belly echoes with battle
with footsteps, with heavy weight with man;
perhaps that is who she is giving birth to. Hymn.

(iv)
I am lighting a candle for Kathleen
who cannot say her own *name*
does not remember its taste, only the scrub of her tongue
across vestry floor
only the washing away of her reflection
the laundries
the disappearing into
steam
into ghosts of women

falling

from grace.

yarls wood[21]

Bedford, 2017

show me a map of your inner arms
so I can see how you got here,
where the borders of your skin are,
where you tunnelled, how you climbed
how the sea was a shouting man
you refused to meet the eye of
with a smile like knuckle
in a room with
a closed door.

[21] Notes in Reference section.

family tree
Blackburn, 1985

There once was a young woman who fed her hair into the jaws of
a small machine, hand held and brittle toothed, the machine was
fingerprint chrome and plastic, its mouth buzzing, its throat full of
wasps; the young woman crouched naked by the socket in the hallway
and plugged her hair in

and with each discarded shard of hair another page destroyed,
burned in the town square, we will warm our palms on the embers of
unwanted hair, another village erased, another man washed right out; I
bet you didn't know:

If you separate a follicle out from the flock, pin it down, deprive it of
human contact, split it open, shine a bright light, and dissect, you will
see that each hair is a tree, and within each tree; is a ringed history,
look:
this is when I first felt my hair was following me
this was when they told me I was not allowed to climb
this is the bike I was forbidden to ride
here is the lesson only for girls
this is needlework   do it
here is a saucepan   stir yourself into it
here is the punch surgically removed from the knuckle
here is you breathing underwater
over there, your father
a flickering perception point
event horizon
a cursor
and here is your mother   this pillar of salt
and here

a daughter not looking back.

dark matter

for invisible queer women everywhere.
The World, Constant

They are not there.
They are not there still.
standing in silent rows,
lines of freshly ploughed smiles
seeded with insolence.

They are not there.
They are not there still.
nursing their blank wombs,
their unwater furrows;
an unwillingness to grow.

They are not there.
They are not there still.
not when they were taken
not when they were dressed
not when they were shaved
not when they were worn
not when they were turned inside out
not when their veins, their double helix
snaked from their wrists
and became chains
to bind one invisible woman
to the other.

They are not there.
They are not there still.

They are not there in Chechnya.
They are not there in Syria.
They are not there in Cambodia.
They are not there in South Africa.
They are not there in America.

They are the space between words.
They are the silence in this conversation.

the
dark matter
from which everything
will be born.

downwind
Portsmouth, 2017

You learn to sit downwind of them
spine angle apology
urban prayer head
sorry
Don't look at the looking, just
curve into woman or
lower voice to raise life expectancy,
chances of work chances of living without a narrator,
do not hold hands
breathe slightly out of register
so that you can hear if the breathing behind
quickens,
soldiers boots,
like Sammy and Chris last winter
don't get the night bus home
don't think about that
but choose the chair in the corner
by the plant that is never watered
marry the door
and laugh when they do

laugh.

the length of a piece of string

UK classroom, Spring 2017

I am wondering whether string is needed or
whether the stitching together begins at birth, umbilical thread,
from a hole into a fraction
from a zero to a 1;
I am wondering if all of this is binary. code.
If a piece of string can stretch from Somaliland to Hackney to
Blackpool to Kabul to home, I
am wondering if the world is wrapped up in string,
if the same twine that seals you binds all women to themselves;

I am wondering which of our mouths is sealed
I am wondering when they stopped speaking to each other.

form poem

Hackney, 2017

your tongues are grey linoleum corridors
lined with waiting women,
you hearts are modular, desk share, tick box tattoos:
you have never seen a woman drowning in wild seas of council flat
carpets,
or felt your stomach become a mouth that eats you. you have never
felt hunger, or shadow or the second grief that follows death
when you cannot give the earth;
you cannot afford to feed the bird-mouths of graves; death is a luxury
around these parts, &

you have never felt something small taken from you & seen it worn
around the neck of another,
or coldness at the climb of your neck as they ask you
to tell them again what it was like
did it hurt
did you fight
you have never been asked to sign your name in any language but
your own
or sold sleep in exchange for pennies dropped onto your children's
eyes
you have never weighed rape against sugar
or sat in a prefabricated bedroom somewhere on the outskirts of
unhappiness
telling a small child
that their father was an invader
a king from another country
and there are now new anthems to learn.

united kingdom, 2017

Support for a child conceived without your consent

Including rape or while you were in a coercive or controlling relationship

Please note there is a separate form for Northern Ireland claimants. This is for England, Scotland and Wales claimants only.

From 6 April 2017 support through Child Tax Credit, Universal Credit or Income Support payments will generally only be available for the first two children you are responsible for. Child Tax Credit will continue to pay for all children born before that date.

For the purposes of this form, by "child" we mean anyone aged under 16, or a young person aged under 20 who enrolled on, accepted or started full-time non-advanced education, such as A-levels, or approved training before they turned 19.

There are exceptions for further children and these are detailed at **www.gov.uk/hmrc/ctc-exceptions**

One of those exceptions applies where either:

- you did not, or could not, consent to the act that led to the conception of the child, or
- you were in a coercive or controlling relationship with the other parent of the child at or around the time of the conception.

In order to get this extra support, you must not be living with the other parent of the child. You will be asked to confirm this in this form.

HM Revenue
& Customs

Department
for Work &
Pensions

NCC1 4/17

Support

rape

through
this
mean
detailed
coercive
controlling
form.

dead name[22]

for Jay and Tane
Burnley, 1985

we slipped out when they were sleeping
my Dead Name, and I.

I awoke
to the feel of the name cold against my cheek
held a mirror to its mouth
and my Dead Name was an 'o'
a nothing
a girl.

I did not call the police or alert the authorities. The truth is, I wanted it to die.

I smuggled Dead Name
wrapped in a bedroom rug
sideways through the front door
nodded at the neighbour
who had never understood my face
and eased Dead Name into the back of
the car. Dead Name's legs stuck out
and would not bend
stiff now
with the act of living.

we drove
Dead Name and I
until the night looked as though it were finally rising up off the land
zipping its trousers
lighting a cigarette
that burned a hole in the sky.

[22] Definition of Dead Name in Reference section.

you cannot understand the
weight of a Dead Name
until you drag it
feet first
rolled in carpet
through a brawl of forest
and gossiping bushes
to a hidden bit, with soft
ground, where a name might be buried.

I have a spot here.
Call it a family plot.
A cemetery of useless things.

Here is my old pink hairbrush, here a cracked porcelain doll
and there my first training bra
curled like a girl
trying to climb out of herself.

I laid Dead Name to rest
beneath a headstone sculpted from
our last conversation
lowered my head
as if in prayer to the
god of impossible things

and the wind
taught me the melody of my name.

crown court[23]

Prestwich, 1978

I put it to you that you are lying
(beneath a brick body/ gravel skin/ broken bottles shatter into tears)

I put it to you that you are lying
(foetal on the cynical bathroom floor/ nursing your dead baby dreams)

I put it to you that you are lying
(on a hospital sheet/ stretched tight as wasp fists/ his smile waiting at the end of the universe)

I put it to you that you are lying
(in wait/ quiet as truth/ dumb as daylight/ exiled from our skin)

[23] Notes in Reference section.

avatar[24]

'but… how do you cope with the way the children look at you?'
Colchester, 2017

I send my smile in first –
teeth barred as late night drinking cemeteries, two bouncers dug deep into newspaper face, I am all pisshead epistles and hand slaps, jokes that I am the punchline to: I have taught my tongue to tap dance, faster faster, go on girl, and I laugh until laughter is a grave dug in wet soil, a polite explosion in a distant land where my name knows me better than you *miss, how do you spell 'no'*? I send my smile in first, *it's okay boys, I've got this*: my teeth a white flag, the unrepentant cliffs of Dover *we'll meet again* I sing as we meet for the first time, and my smile you say, is the border between uncomfortable lands, and I'm smiling in the wrong language again.

Did you pack your face yourself, love?

Look at me. Look. This beautiful ugly, this girl who make up ran from whose hair stands apart from her and points, look at me. look. pretty dirt, inelegant ballet of bad breath, imperfect heart, rupture grin, look: I am falling from my face, my body, a bad neighbourhood, a quick walk through the dark side of town – *I keep my other bodies in the wardrobe/ well fed on dumb and thin/ backs turning from me/ hung from wire necks,* look at me. look.

I send my smile in first –

Fold the arms of my spectacles until they look like my mother, remove my spectacles, I am the spectacle, and my eyes invert, I seed the underskin, I sing the body epileptic, and they stare and it's okay; I would scream obscenities, but I am the obscenity, that brittle thin-lip ugly, old grey face girl, the corner you are afraid to turn, with teeth that have been broken into, a ransacked mouth, my smile a hairline fracture, a split in the bedroom ceiling. Look at

[24] For notes on the poem and my personal story go to Reference section.

me. Look. There is another world glimpsed through this snake tail split in everything caught between the two lights – see? A woman sat unsmiling. Look at me. Look.

My smile has grown tired of my face. Children stare through thick breath windows singing male song, I am exiled to the storage cupboard in a school that wants my words, but not my uncomfortable face. I am sick of true stories

I limp home and the woman on the sofa tells me to stop smiling. That my smile could be a scimitar if I held it correctly/ and perhaps this woman is my left side/ and perhaps this woman is the beginning of time/ my chaos cage/ my heart/ my friend/ all flick-knife Buddha/ and Motherfucker Earth/ and she sees you seeing me/ and her grief makes me beautiful.

I send my smile in first –

We the women of ugly and unexpected, who plan our faces like town centres, whose smiles make dictators flinch, whose thin lips crack like whips taming classrooms of perfect things
we send our unspoilt eyes in, we send our blameless skin, we send our open palms upward, we send our hearts forward/ *over the top, lads/* we send our smiles in first –

because one day we know

the rest of us will follow.

SONGS
OF
UPRISING

landays

London, 2017

Landays are a traditional form of Afghan folk poetry which are chanted or sung. They are not written down but survive as an oral form, passed down the mother's side of the family.

They are comprised of 24 syllables in total, 9 on the first line, and 13 on the second.

The Landay belongs specifically to the women of Afghanistan, and each of their poems are a quiet revolution in a land where women are forbidden to write poetry. They are one of the most extraordinary forms of spoken word, a hummed resistance. The word landay roughly translates into 'short poisonous snake', and that is precisely what they are: irreverent, bitter, sorrowful and above all resistant. I wanted to include newly commissioned Landays in this collection, and so led some poetry workshops with female Afghan refugees at Paiwand, an advocacy organisation working on behalf of all refugees from the region, irrespective of ethnicity.

It was an incredible experience. Moving, inspirational and at times hilarious. This is what real revolution looks like: 7 women who have walked through war, given birth on battlefields, swum through political turbulence to finally walk, heads held high, into a small room in London, crouched over a piece of paper and a plate of highly contested biscuits. Their tenacity, courage and resilience is the essence of warriors and of survivors throughout history. My thanks are not enough.

I have included brief biographies of the writers, in their own words. The majority of these landays were written in Pashto or Dari, and translated by Paiwand themselves. As syllables are lost in translation, I also worked on them to highlight the interpreted poetry.

SAMMAR POPAL

I am from Afghanistan and came to the UK in 2017. I live with my son. I was a teacher, head teacher and school principal in Afghanistan, and have written several volumes of landays in my mother tongue.

What do you want from me, enemy?
You destroyed my house, ate my country and killed my youth

I was born in a war torn country
The whole of our lives we have washed in a rain of tears

Please bring peace to my Afghanistan
Wave goodbye to the fight that has destroyed all our lives

May your red hands shatter, Taliban
The ones you used to rip in half my memories

The Taliban have forbidden love
Every lover is an enemy, every bed war

BASIRA HEEMAT

Basira, 25, left Afghanistan when she was 19. She lives in London with her two young children and volunteers with project admin at Afghan Association Paiwand. In the future she would like to build on her skills and gain employment.

I was born in holy land Mecca
My whole life I have cried like rain storms in the desert

Make peace your pathway, destroy borders
Get rid of segregation, the destroyer of homes

The white sorrow of your wedding night
The tears of the sky fell down on the mother of bride

The stones and plant life were not peaceful
Mountains were spitting fire in sorrow, volcano heart

The birds were crying in the night sky
Each night a new sorrow, each night a new bird crying

    The summer has left and the storms have come
    You were crying like the leaves in Autumn

Darkness drops across the open mouthed world
The sun has turned its back, faced away in bitter shame

    Disappointed you were hurt and left
    Abandoned and no one there to help or to guide you

There was raging fire deep in your heart
But you were melting like a candle into streams of blood

FATEMA S. HAWYDI

My name is Fatema and I have been a refugee for my whole life, therefore I do not know how it feels to have a home. He was my only home, but the war took him. It took my only home.

To be or not to be, no one cares
When death or life looks the same in the refugee camp

    Do you want to be killed or to be killed?
    How come I have never been given a real true choice?

Child protection laws do not apply
Where children can be used as a human shield

    I've always wanted to be a boy
    In a land where that is something you can be proud about

My mum desperately shuts her eyes
She doesn't want to be the mother of a fourth girl child

    Between love and war his love survived
    But she lost it, all of it, between the bombed out cars

Please forgive me for not being there
And please forgive me for not softly holding your hand

The flag is on fire, who cares about the child?
No one reaches through rubble; no love, no hope or smile

RONA HEYDARI

I am from Afghanistan and came to the UK in 2010. I live with my family here. I came to the UK because of war. I am a pharmacist; I hope I can find a job.

God, everyone wants you to give
But I want you to take my fatigue and depression

How long should we mourn humanity?
Even God is tired of endless pain and cries for help

Hand in hand we should always fight on
Until we die we won't stop our battle for freedom

Even my own dreams were restricted
I was forced to complete another man's dream before mine

sea shanty

Blackpool, 1973

(i)

There is a doorway at the end of the corridor.
Behind it is the end of the world.

(ii)

I awoke and the hotel was burning.
my sheets were on fire, flames sang the wallpaper clean off the walls,
and the ceiling hung low in the heat - my mother's belly as she waited
for me to begin - and I leapt to my feet and out of the bedroom,
raced along long tunnels of burn, pirouetting with falling debris, and
- breath an opera of ash - reached the stairway, but the stairway was
made of bones, the spine of it cracked beneath my feet, and I clung
to the edge of everything that had come before and found breath in
my dressing gown pocket, and, hair a conflagration, returned to the
long corridor with its slow applause of doors.

It is important to never leave a burning hotel
without first checking the rooms
for survivors.

(iii)

In the first room, a child my age played etch-a-sketch, drawing
the outline of man she repeatedly rubbed out. I threw her over
my shoulder, the right one, she still clinging to her game and the
certainty of erasure. In the second room an older woman slept
beneath her single bed and would not meet my gaze, until I crawled
down beside her, and together we wrote our names on the under
mattress. In the third room I found myself, sat upright on a bed a
of flames, head buried in the pillow of a burning book, refusing to
look up, to travel back down the alleyways of my eyes - as though she
knew every escape route would lead her back to this room.

All of them I gathered to my chest, confetti children, seeds of things,
and cast them to the bright wind.

(iv)

I am still in the room at the end of the corridor.
It is best that I am left there.
From here
I can hear all of the rooms breathe, and
have learned the language of loss,
the song of uprising.

ansisters

Greenham Common, 1987

these vagabond women
these wrong-haired girls
these walkers along Fallopian roads that curve into names
these sisters of broken teeth
derelict terraces in the rubble of mouths
these flocks of shrieks
these punched laughs
these clutched keys
these copywriters of bed sheets
these rouges of bruises
these deep nights of ugly and beauty and innocence:
see how we birthed the word.
see how we unpicked razor wire perimeters like badly knitted
jumpers
see the smiles bridging our faces
see how we dreamed in different languages
see how we cradled sleeping suffragists in the soft of our fists
see how we danced at the end of the world.
see how we lived in hard houses
see the chill out that kept us warm
see the storm at the edges of eyes
see the thin line we stepped over
and inhaled
that we wore as hangmen's ropes around our necks
See the stain on the wall turn into
the face of your mother
see her smoking
see her clean herself into corners
see her wash herself away
see her rubbed out
haunting you from your polished boots;
see it become brown girls pirouetting from umbilical ropes
strung from the old man's hand of a stripped yew tree
see a picnic at apocalypse
see our gingham grins

see a land beneath a single bed
see women invaded like oil rich countries
see two mouths. neither of them speaking.
see white girls written over
see black women. see black women. see black women.
see the presence of absence
see the mother sewn inside her father
see the child tap dance in a gilded bird cage
see women flicker like neon lights
see a girl catch a bullet in her teeth. and swallow.

these vagabond women
these wrong-haired girls,
who held hands when you could not
and sang songs you had forgotten the words to
and carried you. Carried you.

Our ansisters
Hold them to the light;
on clear nights:

you can see yourself.

concerto for the dead[25]

South Africa July 2013, Germany 1942, Walthamstow 2017

(i) Duduzile Zozo

it was in Brooklyn I met her. she came to me in the steam
from the hotel bath
I've come along way, she mouthed,
in the eye of a whale, on the back of a tic on the wing of a songbird,
in the dead fish of a ship, in the contrail of a plane;
You are writing a book, she asked? I pulled the towel tighter to my chest.
Yes.
She sat on the edge of the bath and sighed. Her breath was ghost.
I have a story for you;
they had watched me for years
as I grew taller than my body, noting
the way I walked like Revelation, each step a swear word, an insult,
profanity, the way
feet meant the earth,
the way dresses fell from me like autumn,
and women smiled when I did
and watching, from their under eye, their overhang look, they shrunk into
the bushland of darker thoughts;
they say animals live there, wild things, that
have tasted freedom
and learned to walk on two feet. Men meet in bars, and hate the day.
they say they lived behind me
all my life
always behind,
and a man does not like to follow.

When they came for me,
they were prayer and animal
their cocks crucifixes

[25] See Reference section for explanation of the names cited throughout poem.

and I lay
corrected.

(ii) Henny Schermann

I see you in the smoke from my cigarette
cocky, one eyebrow raised, your
hair cut as short as life; I seem to think
you were drinking, holding a bourbon or some other distilled masculinity,
a belly of flames
and ash,
lighting your cigarette from mine.
'bones rise', you said, smiling like railway tracks, like
brothel corridors, cheap red velvet lips, your eyes
green badges, we knew they were coming, you said, but
stood our ground, until we became the ground, and when they took her,
the skin fell from my face,
the trees burrowed their heads beneath the soil, and all of the stars
were insignia.

(iii) the ghost beside you on the settee

The children of war rise
closer to home now, in the back of the garden
waking from silent soil beds, materialising by the sides of motorways,
sudden in the
seat opposite you,
pressing into you at rush hour.
they are shouting but we cannot hear them. bombs fall from lips.

The first one came to me at dawn,
her small mouth
a mass grave
cradling the body of childhood: a shoe
an eye caught in awe. a doll with lips like a capsized boat;
she motioned me to follow and I did,
along Quiet Hill where

the birds rarely speak
and there she pointed
back toward the town
black and curled in on itself
a sleeping wolf, amber eyes, smoke tail.
see, she whispered, do you see?

the living haunt the dead.

(iv) this is you

There was a woman I knew who
raised a whole brood of ghost children.
They crowded around the dining table, miming eating. Or played
football in the back yard, their tiny feet
anti-matter.
They kept her awake all night
singing songs their enemies taught them
and in the morning
lined hopefully, neatly, beside her bed
wake up mother, they called, wake up;
the dead are still your children
wake up

and sing.

how to love your self

London, 2012

you are walking through the left side of London when the Past runs into you, at the corner by the train station where young men bottle their faces to sell on the markets later, and women trade teeth for kisses; the Past is standing there, one hand in her pocket, head tilted as if to correct the smirk of reality, scruffy bent boy, smoking that same cigarette you still smoke, thin, bitten into the shape of umbilical. Her eyes don't quite meet yours. How could they?

her best friend is shame and her uncle is fear, she has babysat too many times for the children within men, the pregnant males, and she is ready now, you can see it, she is ready now to walk on. you meet her eyes, and her pupils are long dark corridors at the end of which are closed doors. For a moment, you thought you saw them opening, the impossibility of light, bright butterflies of fire, beginnings.

you notice how much Past has changed. how much more like the Future she looks now. and walk forward into your body.

the legend of our lost tongue[26]

Gutenberg, 1445

'Don't forget: a woman can be happy only with a misogynist.'
—Milan Kundera, *The Book of Laughter and Forgetting*

Remember the legend of your lost tongue

how Hesiod locked it in a bottle the shape of a coffin
how Cicero stole it
how he taught you to fear it
how Foucault made of it a pendulum
that constantly dressed to the left;
how the saints pinned your tongue to the roof of your mouth, with silver pins,
how they gagged it with communion wafer;
how your tongue was a flame
how it blackened, how Hesiod warmed his cold palms by your burning tongue;
how Homer locked it
in a bare room with priapic needlework and a stammering candle
how your hands learned to speak
how the air published you first;
how Ovid made cattle of you
woman comes after the cow
and you grazed at the edges of pages
for centuries,
how Sophocles dressed you in silence and you cried for him. this dark night. this long walk.
how Shakespeare tamed your tongue and made of it a tourniquet to stop the words bleeding;
how Strindberg stripped you naked centre stage. see the woman dance-stupid.
see the puppet girl;

[26] See Reference section for understanding of why these names are included in this poem, a piece about misogyny and literature.

how Tolstoy wrote War and Peace on the skin of his wife
and she is scarred by his constant edits;
how Kerouac inhaled every line you had written;
how Mailer murdered you three times a year
Don't help her. Let the bitch die.
how Ginsberg could not spell woman and drew a hole instead;
how Burroughs used bullets as full stops, how he plucked apples from
deep inside women and swallowed the seeds;
how Orwell freed Man while his wife prepared oysters in another part
of the house
stage left;
how Hemingway hung female trophy heads in his hunting lodge;
how Nabokov named his children. how he named you. how you carry
Nabokov inside you.
how T.S. Eliot could not hear when your name was called
The clock did not stop for you. It ticks still.

all of the gods.
all of the gods.

daughters of the sun[27]

for Khatoon Khider
Iraq, 2016

what it takes to learn a new melody

to fit square edges between soft lips, resplendent with blood, thick
with language, your mouth an orchestra bunker, the symphonies of
Sinjar chaos the mountain: listen.

sing the bombs into birds, the bullets into rain; we have come too
far to return without our daughters. War has its own songs. And you
nodded your head, to the wild thrum of its heart.

A bride remains cooking in the kitchen, her house a confetti of
flames; a daughter bends over writing in the centre of a dust
storm, the faces of her mothers echo the air, a hurricane cradle; a
grandmother pushes an empty swing in the middle of a combat zone
and a mother gives birth on a battleground. All are humming. All are
singing.

There is poetry in handwriting the shape of electrocardiographs
in the turn of escaping women
the meeting of the eye
in the song
ingrown

[27] See Reference section for biography of Khatoon Khider.

commander pigeon[28]

Afghanistan, 2001

This is what will happen if you step on a bird's wing.

The break will heal into war planes
the beak will turn to bullets,
her song a distant siren,
and she will lay war,
perfect round war,
beneath your feet or above your head or
deep inside you
where it will gestate (over months and years and headlines and men
who shoot from mountain tops)
into genocide.

In Mongolia, Golden Eagles tear themselves out of the sun and chase wolves, flocks of iron filings pulled toward magnetic shrieks and, though weightless as peace treaties, bring the wolves down. They dine with bibs tucked into their breasts, and do not speak of it later.

The Shrike is a wily bird, a knowing bird, small with an above average reading age. She hunts alone, plucking feathers and stained glass wings from victims; she eats their flight, before impaling them on thorn bushes. Her larder is well stocked, and the invitations have gone out.

The Moroccan Falcon stuffs other avians into holes, cracks in rocks, so that they cannot escape. She uses her prisoners to teach her daughters how to kill, in a safe and educational environment.

In Afghanistan, Commander Pigeon remembers gravity, remembers her son, and the long way down, the clouds that became him, how feathers would not grow.

[28] See Reference section for biographical context of the woman known as Commander Pigeon.

You don't always kill a bird to eat it.

Sometimes

it is just

to watch

the

fall

old wives' tails[29]

Pendle, Lancashire, 1612

The old bloody witch had a flock of penises grazing in her back garden, behind wire fencing to keep the foxes back, she hand-reared them on seeds of women, tiny beginnings, whole worlds, and some – the favoured ones – she brought into the house itself, let them sit on the sofa beside her, eat at the dinner table, napkins tightly tucked.

But they did not egg. They did not lay, no matter what she fed them.

I remember the old bloody witch, how she culled, saving only one jar of bright chattering cocks on her mantelpiece, which sung when the jar was shaken. I remember sadness as I left a quarter moon in the Sunday cake and my spoon thrilled the bone china; I remember thinking: nothing should be caged stored tamed like this

and so

on a night not unlike this night I broke the jar and set the cocks free

They roam wild now, savage across the moors, muttering in bushes, free range on the streets. All of this. All of it.

is my fault.

[29] See reference section for a brief description of how women were once charged with witchcraft across Europe and the USA, and the consequences of such a charge.

protest song[30]

Cambodia, April 17 1975

mother
forgive us our youth

mother
the song was inside us. forgive us. we walked in symphony. a man learns with his hands. forgive us our youth. we sons wore women like uniforms. forgive us. we sold our sisters on the long walk to the fields. forgive us. masculinity is madness. forgive us. we planted our fathers neck high in fields. forgive us. we stored our mothers in Phnom Penh pantries. forgive us.

mother

forgive our skins of burning books. forgive the night butterflies that rise from the fires. the long march on the backs of our sisters. the spine of the railway. the tide marks around our mouths. the crash of hearts hitting rocks. forgive us our youth.

we were boys then we were men
we thought we could birth a nation
if we ate our mothers
forgive us.

mother
forgive us the gaping of the shops. forgive the looted women. forgive the tapestries of stitched skins. the heads hanging on white walls. the rape of Siem Reap. please. forgive us April 17. that Spring revolution took roots

in our hearts, and the branches wrapped around our tongues, and the fruit that was born was in the shape of grenades –

[30] See Reference notes on the rise of the Khmer Rouge.

the problem with revolution is that it keeps returning. the same song, returning.

we faced our mothers away from us, mother

forgive us
forgive us our youth.

swimming against the song

Libyan Refugee camp, 2015

Men are made of fuck and silver
she said
you must swim against the song
you must learn
that they kill
because they are unsure of what to do with their hands;
because they cannot make
they can only engineer
they cannot pluck apples
she said
there is a snake in the orchard
she said –

I will call my son Apocalypse
and name him after his father.
Our own sons were songs our enemies taught us
she said
shall I give birth to the end of the world?

The whores of war
stand beside us now
she said, with
heavy shaven heads and railway
track ribs;
a Jacob's ladder
for every small soldier who wants to climb the sky
and shake the
hand of God of Allah of Ezekiel of eagles
she said
show us how to un-make the bread of our bodies.
The men are all small soldiers now
Emperors of Nothing
howling into empty rooms
she said

queueing on battle ground conveyor belts toward the open legs of war,
coughing into glinting palms;
men are made of fuck and silver
she said
united in spite of clashing uniform and discordant anthem
against a common enemy
The Common Woman,
and the men march as one
she said
rifles erect
bayonets giggling in the cervical sun
lumen
she said
every woman is a pathway. A border.

And we the women
she said
we the women
sew patches on their trousers
mend flags gashed with holes
stitch papery dresses from religious tracts
and wash and wash and wash.

Men are made of fuck and silver
she said
and kisses
are wounds not yet healed.

cocktail hour
Paris, 1922

Let me tell you, daughter
we the women
wait in corridors and hallways, leading
toward the room
but never in it;
We the women
listening at doors;
We the women, eyes beneath the skirting board
We the women reading maps of discarded clothing, following trails of
apologies fighting
through smokescreens of perfume.

boredom is the greater part of revolution;
they say. I can hardly remember these days.

My cunt barely speaks.
Pucker-lipped and smoking a cerise cigarette yet
silenced not with thread
but with damned faith and etiquette,
with fine bone cakes knitted from psalms.

And yet look closer daughter:
this is not a wine glass in my hand
but a Molotov cocktail;
It is not lipstick on my teeth
but your father
not tights on my legs but nets to cast in seas of thrashing males
this is not a bra but a slingshot
and my heels numchuck.

Keep your head down, daughter.
Keep your smile as wide as your legs.
Curtsey.

Come closer. Here. Any woman who expands beyond the borders of her body is
an insurgent. Any woman who trespasses beyond the boundaries of her body, terrorist.
Starve.

Let me tell you, daughter –
closer
keep your eyes low –
let me tell you
what they never realise
is that it is not our pleasure after all that they remove
not a clitoris at all

but the pin on a grenade.

You are more powerful than you know, daughter.
You know where he lives.

Make him dinner.

the mother of all bombs[31]

Eastern Afghanistan, 2017

The mother of all bombs
is full term now. Empty.
Not knowing it would start like this,
that her children would fall from hurricane womb like this,
small spiralling faces staring unblinking back at her like this,
that they would make
mother-loss below.
Her children
run free through the echoing school yards, the coughing buildings with their heads bent,
bracing; the children of the mother of all bombs play hop-scotch in dust that settles into ghosts,
sing lullabies of loss, siren songs of innocence and smoke. Clap hands, and the
world explodes into butterflies.
a burning child
searches for a womb to climb back into.

The mother of all bombs
watches her babies fall
hoping they will grow up to be
something beautiful. Something rare. Wondering who they will marry, whether
their wives will have faces, whether they will give birth to bombs
too.

[31] Please see Reference section for details.

A telephone rings but no one answers
An answer is given but no one questions
Questions are posed but in empty rooms
Empty rooms scan the skies, and a telephone rings.

(bone) ghosts[32]

Everywhere, Yesterday

and then there was that time you were walking home after a few drinks maybe a cheeky spliff and you didn't live far away so you just said your goodbyes and stepped out into the dark of it and you walked head down maybe widening your stride to look more male less woman and maybe you walked faster than usual and your heels typed your name hard into the concrete as you moved along it then perhaps you slipped your hand into your pocket or handbag and felt for your keys or your deodorant some kind of domestic weapon we are all freedom fighters now and somewhere along the journey your mind drifted and you glanced up at the moon and for a moment you thought you were looking between the legs of God the open legs of God and you thought then how vulnerable even is God.

and you were brought back into your body by your body by the fact of it the idea of it you heard a noise a step or some kind of dragging breathing and you looked around and yes there was a man there and yes you walked faster and harder and were caught in that moment between fear and embarrassment and it's that indecision that will kill us all the in the end and so not wanting to seem impolite un-English you chose not to run but hold your keys as though they were your mother's hand as though they were part of a chain of held hands passed through the matriarchal line from mother to mother stretching back centuries stretching back sentries.

and you reached your door and the man walked past his eyes reading the fine print of the pavement and you wondered as your keys eased into the lock without resistance without compassion if you will always be followed home by (bone) ghosts.

[32] See Reference for definition.

hard brexit[33]

UK, 7 June 2017

Hard Brexit,
firm stiff uncompromising erect Brexit
my country is cock-full,
and silver eye, is withdrawing
without looking,
is wiping itself across Europe,
ejaculating pennies on to the bedside table
cheers, love buy yourself something pretty with this
the national health, perhaps
no soft Brexit here
no limp leaving
no flaccid retreat
just hard
                    hard
                              harder.
Europe is a whore. a woman. and we are done.

[33] Please see Reference for definition of Brexit, and the context for this poem.

beautiful revolutionary[34]

And after the sniper fire and the car
bombs, the incendiary devices beneath school buses, after
black smoke was a fur coat slung around the bare shoulders of the city
we the women
gathered in basements
raised our voices above the song of sirens, and
asked ourselves:

What is the beautiful revolutionary wearing this season?

How do you remove blood from beneath finger nails? How can blood
become varnish?
What are the best ways of keeping your nails unbroken in war?
What are your 5 top tips for removing the smell of burning villages
from hair?

The beautiful revolutionary knows
there is always time for cleansing, especially in the Baltic States,
always time to take a little time to
feel the pull on your stomach muscle, the stretch of the gluteus maximus
as you lift the rifle and aim; and hold. And breathe. Repeat for 10;
you can use the recoil to build your core strength.
How might you best explore the elegance of a bullet proof vest?
What colours do civil unrest come in;
can it be snipped to fit better across the hip, how can war extenuate
the silhouette?
Readers' hot tips to bounce back from helmet hair.
How to keep your revolutionary man well fed, and coming
back for more.
We beautiful revolutionaries wear eyeshadow on our cheeks
blend in with the nothing our city has become;
cataclysm our catwalk,
our eyelashes blackened trees on Kiev streets

[34] Please see Reference section for the context for this poem.

our kohl
the lines around everything else. The line for bread. The line for water.
The line that may never be crossed. The front line.
We have been using our high heels to climb the city walls,
scaling skyscrapers with stilettoes in hand, grappling hooks,
biting pins out of our pneumatic breasts –
take that

counter-revolutionary
take that
and that
and
that.

harder.

fishing for the gulabi gang[35]

Northern India, 2010

we wait in the midnight lift or along the blurred roads the quiet places
where you come to hunt and
we wait for you we know you will come you always come
standing slightly behind your breath a running man in a forest your
shadow a shape cut out of air
you always come with
your swinging grin your soil mouth your fragile your lost.

Come here.

Sampat
is the bait,
her body a hook in the pond-light
and we are the line that pulls them in, we the women
around the corner, we of shadow;
Sampat stands in a skirt as short as temper, her heels a semaphore a lure
raw red lips attract flies
and he comes
as though born of the concrete itself
a bone ghost
walking into the grave of her arms.

Come on. Come and get us.
We are waiting.

[35] Please see Reference section for a description of the Gulabi Gang.

everything you have ever lost

Everywhere, Always

Everything you have ever lost is in here.

(i) she

how the lines on your face were written
how you cannot afford your own face
how your face is a battlefield, deserted
a war between parents
how your pockets are tunnels and you are lost in them
how no one comes even though you call all night
how your call is the sound of something small breaking
how your teeth are tower blocks in which only white ghosts live
how your skin is a lost birth certificate
how your birth certificate is proof of your death
how they stole your smile to store on a high supermarket shelf
how your body was taken from you. how your body was returned
parts missing. batteries no longer included

(ii) he

how the industry unmade you
how your tongue was a conveyor belt
and you could not make the words fast enough
how your soul was kept-well fed in a zoo
how the zoo was a library of lost souls
how the souls stared unblinking from glass enclosures
how the glass was etched with the hieroglyphics of rage
how you made an origami figure of a small boy staring
how some boys cry with their fists

(iii) she

how some girls hang themselves from the thin edge of their smiles
how they told you that white was the colour that contained all others
how your skin became a colour that contained you

how skin becomes insignia
how they sold black back to you
at inflated prices
how rainbows are portents. how rainbows are borders.
how you travelled to the other side of the rainbow and met a stranger travelling back the way you had come
how the stranger looked like you
how you are a stranger

(iv) he

how your mouth is a disused mine
how the mines were dug out with the mouths of your ancestors
how your ancestors were born after you
how you cannot remove the bruise of coal dust from your shoulder
how there is nothing natural about cotton
how cocaine is more honest than cotton
how a length of string stretches all the way from Indian plantations to starling Lancashire mill towns
how smoke rises from mill town chimneys
and you recognise its face.

Everything you have ever lost is in here.

(v) she

how you tattooed your arm with his fingerprints, a memorial
how each fingerprint reminds you of web
how the scar on your belly distils into atlas, a landmine, a treasure;
how they spat at you and the saliva became a sea and you sailed easily across it to the other side of your heart
how your heart was a tectonic plate
how your heart rubbed
how it drifted apart
how other people set up home on the opposite side of your heart to you
how they sent smoke signals
how you answered
how your words turned to ash and blew away

how your voice was thin ice you were afraid to walk across
how silence was a song your enemy taught you
how the last bus home took you to another woman's city
how home keeps moving. how you knocked on the door of your home and a stranger answered
how your father lives in your face
and nowhere else
how you told them you were a woman and they told you there were no more women left, not like you
how you were the last girl
how you married a prison
how he said you were good looking
how they said you were good handwriting
how you were written by someone else
how you no longer fitted your body
how your body no longer fit the mould of the bed
how you said no.
how you said no again.
how no is spelled yes
how you were raped by a high court judge
how the judge's wigs were mushroom clouds floating over the horizon

(ii) he

how your dreams were trained to walk in tight circles
how your dreams were dogs
how you named your dog after the first woman you beat
how you beat her, your bright piñata
so you could build a house of sweets
and eat it
how you learned to walk on women
how women learned to smile at you
how their smiles were tightropes
how their smiles were cut throats
how your father was a bomb
and your mother rich in minerals
how they gentrified your streets
how you were forced out of your own mouth.

(iii) she

how you left your body in a bedroom with purple wallpaper
how your body was a hotel on the edge of a hollow sea
how you understood the language of the sea
and why it keeps returning
how love sat beside you on a broken-backed sofa and changed the channels.
how one hand was all that was required.
how you placed your palm prints beside each other and found they made an atlas that would lead you out of here.
how love woke you
how you fell
and through falling uncovered the archaeology of your wings
how after the grey apocalypse that no one else noticed
you realised that trees hold hands beneath the earth;
how you learned to hold hands beneath the earth.
here is the music of your sister breathing
here is the shape of your mother
here is the shadow that abandoned you
here is your unfound song
here is the legend of your lost tongue
here are your teeth. Your womb. Your bone

everything you have ever lost is in here.

and it is waiting
to come home.

exorcism

Dalston, 1997

It is 3am on balls pond road
The moon is a mirror ball and the constellations are peeling sequins/
night birds screech and flutter/ lips flicker/ feather boas twitch/
inside they are playing house/ music/ *you be mother*/ but outside
I am leaned over by the bins at the back of the pub/ she's gone
now/ better for everyone/ and nausea has risen like hemlines/ like
empires/ and my stomach is a fist punching a small child over my
lips and onto the damp pavement.
The child finds legs/ and whispers them into walk. She stands and
faces me. Her eyes are long corridors/ in a derelict seaside hotel/on
the edge of everywhere/ and at the end of it a door begins a slow
applause/ open and shut/ open and shut/ whore's thighs/ and I
walk to the end of the hallway/ and enter the room/ and behind the
closed open door/ is the end of the world:
It is Wednesday/ early evening/ and we are a gaggle of young
things/ six or seven years old/ grins banging together as we
giggle-trip toward home/ across the wasteground/ and you were
telling me something that I have forgotten/ so I didn't see the men
approaching/ I never see the men approaching/ until they were
monoliths in front of me/ manoliths/ and this is where I forget/ my
name/ this is where I can remember that the sky was a child's grey
face/ that the scrub grass was talking about us/ that there was an
equal distance between the road and the house/ that we are in the
centre of nothing/ and the bucket/ after the things that I cannot
remember I remember the bucket/ this is the thing I want to forget/
it is the only thing I can remember/ the bucket/ the bucket/ white/
was filled with an avalanche of spiders/ thin as lips/ pleading arms/
a sinking ship/ some things are difficult to remember and harder to
forget.

I don't know why they chose her/ or if she was me/ I don't know
why they pour the spiders/ under her t-shirt/ across her skin/ and
made children crush them. I cannot remember her scream/ but I
recognise the wind when it visits in winter/ fear is small and round/
a stone/ a full stop/ fear is curled/ I cannot remember her scream

but I recognise the wolf when it leaves town and looks back once.

On balls pond road/ someone calls my name/ and for a brief moment/ I remember it/ my stomach a slow fade to black/ I am full of empty/ and the child has run into the guttering.

I am tired of throwing myself up on street corners. The door to the bar opens like the arms of a distant relative I met once in a crowded room/ I smile/ enter/ and women cheer.

hysteria – the wandering womb[36]

Vienna, 1885

(i)
her uterus
that old goat's head
the devil itself
sits whispering
within each woman
waiting for its chance

to sing.

(ii)
My mother told me once of the night
her womb first went wandering,
crawled out of her belly
and dragged itself across the sheet
leaving a trail of mistakes behind.
It disappeared for a moment, then
she saw it
silhouetted at the window
by the light of a cervical moon.
my mother told me
her womb was singing to it.

all night it called.

(iii)
There was another night, she said, when
her womb had gone wandering again.
This time she couldn't see it in the
window,
but heard its thump

[36] Please see context in Reference section.

as it slid down the stairs
and the slam of the door behind it.
The womb did not return for hours.
My mother sat by that same window waiting,
calling to her womb.
When it finally returned
the womb had lipstick smeared against its collar
in the shape of a gun
and smelled
like lightning.

(iii)
Animal within
animal
our wombs paw at the hard earth of our bellies, drought dust
rising into the spirits of human guides
who herd the escaping wombs back home
back
back
into the belly
of the beast.

(iv)
My mother and I both know
there is a place
out there
where all the wandering wombs meet
and discuss practicalities, politics and the poetry
of breathing.
maybe it is a field.
maybe they are seeds.
They shake their heads and comfort each other
Not long now, they sing, not long

and we will be free.

the geography of fury[37]

Xaltianguis, Mexico, 2015

Tonight I will rape a man.

I will wait for him in the darkened alleyway of his dirty mouth
and drug him with promises
and gag him with newspaper rubble
inseminate him with internet
and blue map his skin with my fingerprints,
the cartography of lies,
tracing the journey from a small Indian village where used girls are
strung from tree branches at midnight like condoms
past rows of cracked vases cradling female foetuses buried in the
mammalian hills of Pakistan,
across the wet valleys of Lancashire,
and watch as
a late night train crawls past, last carriage as empty as her eyes.

I will rape him at the back of the bus
and you will laugh
and film his soul leaving the safe house of his mouth –
bags abandoned –
and pin its wriggle to the fluttering pages of Facebook;
like share retweet.

I will rape him in the classroom
and you will clap, take delicate notes on the aesthetics of rape,
as he struggles to escape the bars of my fingers.
I will rape him at the party
and you will dance to the rhythm of his tears,
straighten your smile like the hem of your skirt
and wait for your turn

I will rape him in England.

[37] Please see context in Reference section.

I will rape him in Calcutta.
I will rape him in Saudi Arabia.
I will rape him in Gethsemane.
In Mecca.
In Jerusalem.
In the Vatican.
I will rape him in Washington.
In Paris.
In London.
I will rain rape upon him over the desolate shifting skins of Iraq
Of Syria
Of Turkey
Of Palestine -
he will feel the apartheid of my kiss
the geography of my fury –

I will rape him black.

He will taste the cold walk home,
the knife glint of laughter.
His father will forget his name.
Cars will turn to creeping cats behind him.
Cameras will become enemies,
poetry an apology.
The ground will be ashamed of him.
His skin will be torn clothing in a ditch,
at the side of the road, beneath a shallow bed
and his mother will eat him.

I will rape him in the police station
clutching coffee as thin as integrity
in front of reflective glass, a zoo animal,
and witnesses though next to him will see nothing
but his low neck line
the strait jacket of his smile
his too short jeans.

I will rape him in court

and the judge will rape him too
and the reporters will rape him, stroking spunking pens,
and the television will watch
pleasuring itself
Get over it, son, move on, let go.

I will walk him down the fallopian linoleum fluorescent corridor that
smells of thin cigarettes and mashed potatoes
to a small badly painted room at the heart of him
where a weak and tired bed crouches against a wall that no one
believes in.

And I will wrench the clutched keys from his snapping fingers
and use them to lock him tightly within the prison of his skin
and leave him with the encephalogram of my retreating footsteps
awaiting visitors too embarrassed to knock
and then
and then

and then

I will sit down.
pour us both a drink.
birds will remember the words to their songs.
and I
will move
on.

anthem

The World, 2017

down below women are harvested
their ornate painted carcasses weighed and sold, the gold
in their teeth, smelting into chains
inset with diamonds
necklaces with double helix combinations
forged by global gendercidal corporations –
Abattoirs of Beauty;
small girls are paraded half naked in digital markets
leaning slightly more forward
to the right to the right
each breath bottled, and sold
diluted and sold again
the good thing about women/ is that inside them/ there are more women
it is supply and demand wet dream ghost erection
buy selection boxes of children
click once for no, hit like
to the right to the right
white male judiciary have set up court rooms in your womb, sister
suspend all visas
you may not enter your own body
unless you can prove that you speak the same language
that you know the words to the anthem
while politicians ride rafts of women floating on the financial market
misogyny is big money
women are currency around here;
your womb a goat head the devil the centre of the apple
your blood
the tears of God;
our religious leaders are atheists, pious pornographers
our mothers are martyrs
black canaries beneath blue shrouds
while poets are given typewriters of sand
and songs burrow beneath the skin
ingrown.

But there are girls who wear the birth marks of birds
and mothers who carry their children in their teeth
and women who have tunnelled into themselves and broken free
there are tappings against cell walls of skin
there are notes passed between strangers
hidden beneath jumpers
there are glances inherited, these family heirlooms
there are sigils scribbled in stiletto at the edges of kerbs
there are warnings
there are murmurs
there are scars that begin to speak
there are birds escaping ornamental rib cages

let your poems break free of the aviaries

there are books written on the underside of eyelids
there are lovers
with Morse code kisses
passing secrets
between relay lines of invisible women
and this child ready to give birth to her mother.

You will hear our anthem in the quiet revolution of the kitchen
you will hear it in the metronome of alone
you will hear it hummed sonata by the school gates
in the applause of cubicle doors
the shriek of alive.

You will hear it.

and you will sing

un-broken

Canterbury, 2017

today you are unbroken
walking backward into a room
and returning his kisses
unopened
you are folding his fist like origami butterflies
and setting each fist free through a first floor window, today
you are walking into the punch
and swallowing it whole,
you are
gestating it for
nine long years
until it is born into your
palms
and you are unbroken
unflinching
unmarked

teaching your hands
how to fly.

#meninist #notallmen

The Internet. Now.

█ Mar 11
Feminists and sheep are fucking boarder (sic) line retarded #menist

█ May 7
Shut Up, Feminist #Menist

█ Mar 8
@GMA Women's march is dumb. They will effect the economy in a neg way. Not making money, to circulate it, is dumb. #Menist

█ Mar 8
Feminists go on about equal rights but where's international men's day?

█ Feb 11
because men are the backbone of this country, without men you wouldn't even be allowed to use Twitter #menist

█ 3h3 hours ago
Don't come around me with bossychick, feminism & stuff. I'll break your feather & render you useless like the way you fuck bitches are.

█ 7h7 hours ago
You can support women and be against feminism.

█ Apr 25
Women belong in the kitchen not in the Oval Office thank god that didn't happen @HillaryClinton #fuckfeminism

█ 39m39 minutes ago
The international Slut Scale (in ass-cending order) is as follows: Tart, Slapper, Skank, Trollop, Slut, Whore, Cum dumpster, The Kardashians

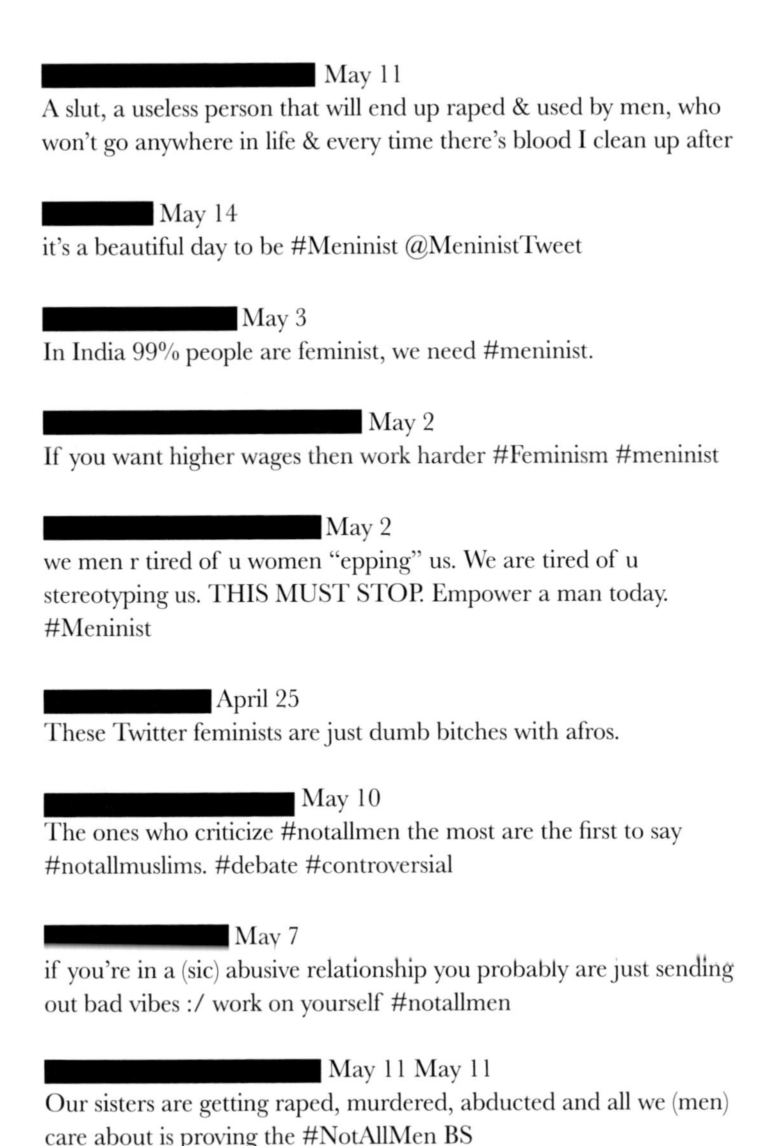

May 11
A slut, a useless person that will end up raped & used by men, who won't go anywhere in life & every time there's blood I clean up after

May 14
it's a beautiful day to be #Meninist @MeninistTweet

May 3
In India 99% people are feminist, we need #meninist.

May 2
If you want higher wages then work harder #Feminism #meninist

May 2
we men r tired of u women "epping" us. We are tired of u stereotyping us. THIS MUST STOP. Empower a man today. #Meninist

April 25
These Twitter feminists are just dumb bitches with afros.

May 10
The ones who criticize #notallmen the most are the first to say #notallmuslims. #debate #controversial

May 7
if you're in a (sic) abusive relationship you probably are just sending out bad vibes :/ work on yourself #notallmen

May 11 May 11
Our sisters are getting raped, murdered, abducted and all we (men) care about is proving the #NotAllMen BS

References

Songs of Silence

My Father, The Lord of War – Serbia's most notorious war criminal, Zeljko Raznatovic aka Arkan and his army the Serbian Volunteer Guard, nicknamed Arkan's Tigers. The poem was inspired by an article about his daughter, who has restyled herself as a socialite in the vein of the Kardashians.

Skin Cells – there has been an 85% increase in the number of women imprisoned in the UK since 1998, a trebling of the figure. Over 53% of those women imprisoned report having being sexually assaulted either as children or a young women, and 46% report being the victims of domestic violence. As a part of the masterclass tour I worked with two women's prisons, with the aim of passing the skills these women need to be able to write their life stories, and through writing and telling them, finally own the events that had – in many cases – brought them to the prison gates. There is a direct correlation between those who are sexually abused as children and those who commit crime as vulnerable adults. Benzo is a fictitious character, a composite of many of the women I have worked with in the judicial system over the last decade.

First They Separate the Men from the Women – when the Maoist revolutionary Khmer Rouge took control of Cambodia in 1975 they created a list of those people who would be suspect by the new state, and who could be executed or imprisoned without trial. As always in revolutions (good or bad) the women are the first to suffer. Their suffering is frequently undocumented.

Pub Street – Pub Street is the famous tourist street in Siem Reap Cambodia. This is the heart of the sex industry in Cambodia, and Western men gather in the bars that line the road looking for young girls, women and in some cases young boys too. The girls and women wear red to make them easily identifiable. I spent an uncomfortable evening with friends watching an older white man dine with two women. When one looked around at me, I saw that she was barely into her teens.

Fuck You's – haikus made up of actual descriptions and words in sex trafficking online sites.

Event Horizon – as a part of the masterclass tour I worked with a group of young girls in a Bristol secondary school who were at risk of being affected by female genital mutilation (FGM). FGM, sometimes known as female circumcision, is an invasive and highly damaging operation of the female sexual organs, including cliterodectomy, excision of clitoris or labia, cutting, scraping, cauterising, and infibulation. The damage caused by these illegal and often insanitary operations includes loss of sexual pleasure, extreme pain during birth, chronic infections and death. It is estimated that more than 200 million girls and women have undergone FGM in 30 countries where the practice is documented. There are an estimated 3 million girls at risk of undergoing FGM every year. The majority of girls are cut before they turn 15 years old. According to NSPCC there are approximately 137,000 girls affected by FGM in the UK.

Marching Song – Leshia Evans is a solitary black woman who faced a line of heavily armed white riot police in a Black Lives Matter protest in Baton Rouge. She was arrested and taken into custody. Four Nottingham #BlackLivesMatter protesters were arrested for willfully obstructing the highway during an international day of peaceful demonstration against racism. An English Defence League protest the following day closed down the city and train station, costing the taxpayer approximately £200,000. No arrests were made. Marching Song is a poem about intersectionality, and how even the most politically conscious of us as white people negate or underestimate the reality of the black experience. White skin has the luxury of protest and demonstration; black skin is either unnoticed or crossed out.

Homs Sweet Homs – at the time of writing there are approximately 4.89 million Syrian refugees, 65 million forcibly displaced peoples and 21 million refugees globally, most escaping conflict or persecution in their homelands. Of that number, approximately half are women. It is worth bearing in mind that most of those who are able to flee their home countries have the money available to pay for their passage. The women often do not have access to financial resources, and so they stay behind, building homes out of the rubble.

God is an Atheist – it is difficult to find a religion that does not denigrate women, both symbolically and in real terms. The Abrahamic faiths (Christianity, Islam, and Judaism) blame women for the Fall of Man and this 'original sin' is used to justify extreme acts of misogyny ranging from professional and societal exclusion to rape and murder.

Letters Home – at least 20.9 million adults and children are currently being bought and sold worldwide into commercial sexual servitude, forced labour and bonded labour. Women and girls make up 98% of victims of trafficking for sexual exploitation. Sex trafficked girls from Vietnam are taken first of all to China. Thousands of young girls and women are trafficked for sex across Vietnam but poor crime statistic reporting means it's difficult to determine an accurate figure. This is the original quote that inspired the poem. *'He took me to the pig slaughter house where he worked and locked me in a dirty smelly cell. Then he came back with six other men. They all, one by one, raped me; one man raped me twice. After a whole night of gang rape I felt faint with pain. When the morning came I heard the workers preparing to start their work. I heard the pigs being pushed into the pens, they were screaming. I knew what that feeling was like – I was no better than the pigs to these men; they could have killed me. Something inside me did die, and I will never be the same. I am twenty-four years old and my life has been like this since 1993.'* I have also had the privilege of working over a number of years with women who have escaped sexual exploitation.

360 – news headlines relating to women across the world in one 24 hour period. I have used the words as they appear with slight alterations, and constructed my own headlines. This is a kind of anti-poem, the poetry being in the concept rather than the writing. A point of connect and context for the book.

Invisible Women – the history of masculine women is erased worldwide. In every culture the lesbian is both the visible and invisible in the same moment. When we are erased from history and ideology it is easy to erase us from life as well.

The Old God – for the New God of Patriarchy and Capitalism to exist, the Old God needed to be symbolically rounded up and humiliated, defeated in Heaven as on Earth. Before the rise of Christianity, people worldwide worshipped a pantheon of gods, both male and female. In *When God Was A Woman* (Merlin Stone, 1976) the author discusses a time when the Mother symbol was widely worshipped, and the world was a 'peaceful, benevolent matriarchal society' until Goddess-reverent traditions (including Ancient Egypt) were attacked, undermined and ultimately destroyed by the ancient tribes, including Hebrews and later the early Christians. They replaced The Old God (the Mother) with the New God (the Father), and the story of misogyny began.

Songs of Survival

Colony – how it feels to not own your body, for it to be an outpost of Someone Else.

The Night Butterflies – a sequence of poems describing my personal story of escape into the underground queer women's culture of 90s London. The sequence explores the idea of the masculine woman, difference, dissonance and our private revolutions on the dancefloor and in the drug chill out zones that took over from our feminist consciousness-raising sessions of the 80s; we stopped passing speculums, and started passing spliffs. We did not stop at changing our relationship to our bodies, but took the fight outward and challenged the entire world to reconsider its shape.

The Hole of Us – following the homophobic massacre at Pulse Nightclub, a newspaper printed a photograph of the first person killed. K.J Morris was the security on the door that night. She looked like me, and it is rare that I get to see images of women who look like me in the mainstream media. She was only visible once she had died.

Free Speech – notes on women's names in poem (source: Amnesty International). Thailand: Sirikan Charoensiri, a 31-year-old lawyer, who is a leading member of Thailand's civil society, faces 15 years' imprisonment under charges of treason and violating a ban on 'political' assembly of five or more persons. Philippines: Senator Leila de Lima, a former justice secretary and former chair of the Philippine Commission on Human Rights, has been recognised as the most prominent critic of President Rodrigo Duterte and his bloody 'war on drugs'. Amnesty said de Lima, 58, had been arrested on politically-motivated charges to silence her. Burma (Myanmar): Wai Wai Nu, under the country's military government, Wai Wai Nu, her two siblings and parents were prisoners of conscience imprisoned by the country's military government. Amnesty pointed out in 2005, the family was shown to a closed-door room, where there was no lawyer present and they were not allowed to speak, to be 'tried' and convicted; Vietnam: Trần Thị Nga, the land rights activist and pro-democracy advocate from Hà Nam province was arrested in January under Article 88 of the Vietnamese Penal Code for 'spreading propaganda against the state', a provision 'regularly used to jail dissidents for lengthy periods'.

Men Who Live Beneath Bridges 1 – working with Traveller girls one day a young women showed me a photograph of a murdered child that has been sent to her over social media. She also let me view some of the worst comments on her page from country (non-Traveller) men, including one that explained what he would do with her babies.

Men Who Live Beneath Bridges 2 – video emerged of a bouncer in Liverpool assaulting a very drunk young woman after she tried to slap him. Social media responded. The poem is made up of are comments made (and re-made by me) after the news was released on a friend's profile page.

Mass – (1) Approximately 10,000 women passed through the Magdalene Laundries in the Irish Republic between 1922 and 1996, a huge mass of women used for free labour, and subjected to religiously justified torture. The Laundries were industrial schools in which the girls were expected to work without payment and without knowing when they might be released. Some of the girls were sent to the Laundries for being pregnant out of wedlock (whether that was by consent or, more commonly, by rape), others because they were the daughters of unmarried women, some because they were orphans, and still more taken from parents or guardians who were unable to look after them. They are sometimes referred to as Ireland's Disappeared. Many of the children born in the nurseries did not survive and were buried in mass graves on the Laundry grounds. Some of the pregnant girls still do not know what happened to their children. Now recognised as a human rights violation and state sponsored torture, compensation is available. (2) Mary Magdalene Laundries – named after the first 'fallen woman'. (3) UN Committee Against Torture: 'gravely concerned at the failure by the State party to protect girls and women who were involuntarily confined 'in the laundries.' This piece is deeply personal to me and my family, and is dedicated to Kathleen, who experienced the Magdalene Convents first hand.

Yarls Wood – an immigration detention centre for women seeking refuge or asylum in the UK. Women are held here indefinitely without charge.

United Kingdom – Form NCC1 4/17: the so called Rape Clause issued by the British HMRC. It is now a legal requirement that a woman prove her child was conceived under duress (rape or coercion) in order for her to claim support for that child's upkeep. This is an example of a black-out poem, where the original text is erased to allow the poem to float to the surface, in their own words.

Dead Name – the name given to someone according to their designated sex at birth. This poem is a funeral for that name.

Crown Court – In 2015–16, police recorded 23,851 reports of adults being raped – nearly all of them women – compared with 10,160 in 2011–12, according to data released by HM Inspectorate of Constabulary on behalf of its rape monitoring group. 80 per cent of cases do not get to the prosecution stage. This poem is a fictionalised account of those women's testimonies that do enter the judicial system. *Avatar* – masculine women find it difficult simply to walk down the street without attracting comment. I call this 'living with my narrator'. This poem is about how I deal with this prejudice and constant commentary in my work delivering masterclasses in schools, and is dedicated to one school in particular, where these events are set.

Songs of Uprising

Concerto for The Dead – (1) South African lesbian Duduzile Zozo was raped and murdered in a corrective attack. He raped her with a toilet brush. One man stood trial for her rape and murder, though others were suspected of being involved (2) Henny Schermann: Henny was arrested in a lesbian bar in NAZI Germany by gestapo in 1940, and was taken to a brothel and then on to Ravensbruck where she and her partner were gassed. On her report they described her as a 'Licentious lesbian'.

The Legend of Our Lost Tongue – misogyny within literature, both classical and contemporary, that features the degradation of or complete erasure of women. This is a poem about loss, that moment when the reader realises that her literary hero either hates her gender or simply cannot see them as humans of equal agency, reason and power.

Daughters of the Sun – Khatoon Khider is a Yazidi woman, and a famous folk singer before the rise of ISIS. In the horrific attack on and massacre of the Yazidi people in Sinjar August 2014, many women were taken forcibly by Daesh and have been sold to individuals and sex traffickers, while others have been taken to rape camps. On her escape, Khatoon Khider formed an army of women called Daughters of the Sun. They are military trained and are waiting to be sent to the front line. According to Daesh's understanding of Islam, to be killed by a woman will prevent a man from entering Heaven; a small revenge.

Commander Pigeon – Afghanistan's only known female warlord is Bibi Ayisha, nom de guerre: Commander Pigeon, so named because 'she killed with the elegance of a bird.' According to articles written about her, Soviet forces murdered her son and it was this horrific event that encouraged her jihad, fighting against government forces. She is said to control major drug trafficking routes in the region and is by all accounts a terrifying human being. I have used the violent bird imagery here (pretty much based on truth) to cut across the usual interpretation of the bird symbol.

Old Wives' Tails – the witch hunts across Europe and America claimed the lives of 888 women, most of whom were political prisoners of their time, women who lived on the margins of society, or who owned property that landowners wanted. It is generally agreed that the hunts were also a vital part of the Christian mission to dominate all aspects of life, and especially the lives of women. Preposterous lies were created to justify the hanging or burning of the women, including that they spoilt crops, that they kept penises in jars, that they cursed men into impotency, or that they visited men at night as succubus. There was a strong sexual element to the trials themselves, including the public stripping and torturing of the women.

Protest Song – The Khmer Rouge were a Maoist inspired revolutionary army led by Pol Pot that took over Cambodia on April 17 1975.
The revolution which forced men and women to leave the cities and work in the fields, led to the deaths of around 1.4 million people. It is the clearest example of indoctrination in action. Women were forced into marriages and sold to high ranking officials.

The Mother of All Bombs – on 13 April 2017 President Donald Trump ordered the MOAB, the largest non-nuclear ordinance ever used, to be dropped on Nangarhar in Afghanistan in an attempt to kill suspected ISIS terrorists in tunnels beneath the town. It devastated the region and it is estimated that 96 Daesh members were killed. The number of civilians killed in collateral damage are at this stage unknown. At the time of the bombing I was working with refugee women from the area, who had family and friends still trapped there but they were unable to contact them. I cannot imagine this level of state sanctioned grief and despair on a daily basis. The women I was working with were all mothers.

(Bone) Ghosts – definition: bone ghosts (i) are the ghosts grown from your own body due to past experiences (ii) ghosts of family members (iii) are memories of things that have not happened yet (iv) DNA

Hard Brexit – the masculine based sexualisation of the UK Referendum on Leaving Europe, June 2016 and the whole of the Alt Right political agenda. The Alt Right agenda, like the NAZI propaganda of the 1930's, bases its publicity on notions of heterosexual virility, and the strong potent white male.

Beautiful Revolutionary – Elle magazine, reporting on the Ukrainian Revolution, Feb 2014: 'We turned into a kind of civil female front. Our hair smells of smoke and fumes ingrained in our fingers. It's probably ugly, not fashionable, or trendy. But we never felt more confident. And, as you know, when you feel confident – you are beautiful.' 'My friends email me, telling me how they have replaced their purses with Molotov cocktails, their heels with helmets, and their jackets with bullet proof vests–the city has become a war zone.' 'and in my free time I cooked national Ukrainian soup "Borscht" with my girlfriends to bring to the combat zone to feed the fighters.' Even in the midst of fierce fighting, a woman must understand her role, her gender construct.

Fishing – there are many female vigilante gangs operating informally across the world, often rising from regions in which women are targeted for rape and murder, while the State does little to protect them. In Mexico a group of women formed a movement called Women of the Xaltianguis Citizen Police, an unofficial (and far more effective) police unit, who ride on pickup trucks and patrol the most dangerous areas armed with guns, offering safety to women travellers in the area.

Hysteria – 'In the middle of the flanks of women lies the womb, a female viscus, closely resembling an animal; for it is moved of itself hither and thither in the flanks, also upwards in a direct line to below the cartilage of the thorax, and also obliquely to the right or to the left, either to the liver or the spleen, and it likewise is subject to prolapsus downwards, and in a word, it is altogether erratic. It delights also in fragrant smells, and advances towards them; and it has an aversion to fetid smells, and flees from them; and, on the whole, the womb is like an animal within an animal.' Aretaeus, 2nd century AD. Hysteria is the first mental disorder attributed solely to women, and consisted of the idea that the 'wandering womb' created disruption and rebellion within women. Freud developed the idea to consider that hysteria may be the result of a suppressed traumatic experience, again largely found in women.

The Geography of Fury – a reversal poem, in which the poem reimagines the victim as the male. I use the word rape repeatedly as I want to press home the shock of the word. It is also a poem about rage and impotence, and the continual suggestion from dominant ideology that those affected by rape simply 'move on.' For the purposes of this poem I mixed in ideas about the Gulabi Gang of North India, a group of women who publically and often physically attack rapists and sex offenders.

#meninist, #notallmen – the male power answer to feminism and sexual politics. NotAllMen, similar to AllLivesMatter is a movement designed to silence feminist deconstruction of contemporary reality. The tweets here are taken directly from social media, and included to provide some context to the collection.

Acknowledgements

The title of this book is taken from an article about the Khmer Rouge in Cambodia by Sophiline Cheam Shapiro in *Children of Cambodia's Killing Fields.*

The poem 'Canto' was commissioned by She Growls for an anthology of women writers edited by Carmina Masoliver, out now on Burning Eye Books.

This book arose from a conversation with the poet and editor Anthony Anaxagorou. He was the first person to hear the 'Canto' poem aloud, and encouraged me to consider creating an entire book based around it. It was his idea to expand the poems outward from my own experience, and his continual support, advice and love that has made me want to write it.

Special thanks to Sabrina Mahfouz, who has worked as Content Editor on this book, and who guided me through the ideas and possible avenues of research. There is no one else who I could have asked to guide me along these tricky tributaries, no one else who I knew would stop me if I walked too far. Thanks.

Major gratitude to Tom MacAndrew for producing the project and for daring to enter the portal alone, and to Pete Read who designed the whole of my website, and added the blog page allowing me to publish women online myself.

Thanks to all the women I have met on this journey, either in masterclasses or in interviews, all of whom contributed to the feeling that this project could work. You can check out their poetry via www.joelletaylor.co.uk – and submit your own for consideration too.
Huge thanks to Arts Council England for funding this project, and in particular, Sarah Sanders for initial advice that led to the development of the masterclass programme.

Thanks to:

The family: Marie Seary, James and Megan Rose, Fergal Rose Taylor, David Taylor, Rose Hawley and Jade and Jason Hawley, to Queenie, Ishmael and Souley.

The other family: Out-Spoken Crew - Karim Kamar, Sam 'Junior' Bromfield, Assumpta Ozua, Tom MacAndrew, and all the quiet collaborators.

The agents of everything good: Thomas Kareem Crosbie and the Pace Foundation, Maggie Crosbie, Kayo Chingonyi, Bernardine Evaristo, Sisters Uncut, Paiwand, Siblings Together, BoomSatsuma, Workers of Art, Safe Ground, HMP Send, HMP Downview, Wise Words Festival, Beth Cuenco, Andy Willoughby, Bob Beagrie, Electric Kool Aid Cabaret, Teesside University, Danny Pandolfi, Alya al-Sultani, People of the Road, the Poetry Society, Apples and Snakes, MIMA, Alex Vellis, inspire self-healing, Burning Eye, and all those who helped develop this project.

The women poets who founded the current UK scene: Salena Godden, Patience Agbabi, Malika Booker, Zena Edwards, and Joolz.

This book is dedicated with love and honour to the magical Marie Seary, who works hard to help women globally remember their stories, and who helped me remember this. To find out more about her work go to www.inspireselfhealing.com

Bio

Joelle Taylor FRSA is an award-winning poet, playwright and author. She is anthologised widely and is included as a Subject for Study on the OCR GCSE paper. She has performed both nationally and internationally and was recently long listed for the Jerwood Compton Poetry Fellowship. She founded the SLAMbassadors youth slam in 2002 for the Poetry Society, making it the longest running spoken word education and development programme in the U.K, and remains its Artistic Director. As a part of the research for this book she led a number of masterclasses with diverse groups of women including those in prison, those affected by FGM, Afghan women refugees, traveller women, LGBT groups, those in recovery from domestic violence, and survivors of sexual abuse. She is the host of Out-Spoken, London's premier night of poetry and music.

Other titles by Out-Spoken Press:

Stage Invasion: Poetry & the Spoken Word Renaissance
Pete Bearder

The Neighbourhood
Hannah Lowe

Nascent
Vol 1: A BAME Anthology

Ways of Coping
Ollie O'Neill

A Greek Verse for Ophelia & Other Poems
Giovanni Quessep

The Games
Harry Josephine Giles

To Sweeten Bitter
Raymond Antrobus

Dogtooth
Fran Lock

How You Might Know Me
Sabrina Mahfouz

Heterogeneous, New & Selected Poems
Anthony Anaxagorou

Titanic
Bridget Minamore

A Silence You Can Carry
Hibaq Osman

Email:
press@outspokenldn.com